Creating Teams with an Edge

The Harvard Business Essentials Series

The Harvard Business Essentials series is designed to provide comprehensive advice, personal coaching, background information, and guidance on the most relevant topics in business. Drawing on rich content from Harvard Business School Publishing and other sources, these concise guides are carefully crafted to provide a highly practical resource for readers with all levels of experience. To assure quality and accuracy, each volume is closely reviewed by a specialized content adviser from a world-class business school. Whether you are a new manager interested in expanding your skills or an experienced executive looking for a personal resource, these solution-oriented books offer reliable answers at your fingertips.

Other books in the series:

Finance for Managers
Hiring and Keeping the Best People
Managing Change and Transition
Negotiation
Business Communication
Managing Creativity and Innovation
Managing Projects Large and Small
Manager's Toolkit

HARVARD
BUSINESS
ESSENTIALS

Creating Teams with an Edge

The Complete Skill Set to Build
Powerful and Influential Teams

Harvard Business School Press | *Boston, Massachusetts*

978-1-59139-290-3 (ISBN 13)

Library of Congress Cataloging-in-Publication Data

Harvard business essentials : creating teams with an edge :
the complete skill set to build powerful and influential teams.
p. cm. — (The Harvard business essentials series)
ISBN 1-59139-290-X
1. Teams in the workplace. I. Title: Creating
teams with an edge. II. Series.
HD66.H3763 2004
658.4'022—dc22
2003019405

Contents

Introduction   **xi**

    What's Ahead   xiv

1   Team Concepts   **1**

    Understand These First

    Why Teams?   5

    Do You Really Need a Team?   7

    Benefits and Costs   7

    Making the "Team Versus No-Team" Decision   8

    Summing Up   10

2   Essentials for an Effective Team   **13**

    The Foundation of Success

    Competence   14

    A Clear, Common Goal—With Performance Metrics   15

    Commitment to a Common Goal   17

    Every Member Contributes—Every Member Benefits   20

    A Supportive Environment   21

    Alignment   22

    Summing Up   24

3   Forming the Team   **25**

    The Crew and Its Charter

    Team Sponsor   27

    Team Leader   29

    Team Members   31

Facilitator   39
The Team Charter   39
Aligning Behavior Through Rewards   42
Summing Up   43

4 Getting Off on the Right Foot   45
Important First Steps

Host a Launch Meeting   46
Decide About Decisions   49
Plan and Schedule the Work   52
Define the Measures of Success   56
Develop a Budget   57
Create Integrating Mechanisms   58
Establish Norms of Behavior   62
Summing Up   64

5 Team Management Challenges   67
Where Leaders Matter

The Leader's Role   68
Encouraging Team Identity   76
Guarding Against Groupthink   80
Managing Team Creativity   82
Managing Conflict   86
Summing Up   89

6 Operating As a Team   91
Putting Ideas to Work

Keeping an Eye on Team Processes   92
Winning One Bite at a Time   98
Supporting Team Learning   100
Evaluating Performance   103
Summing Up   106

7 The Virtual Team   107
A Collaborative Challenge

Benefits and Challenges   108
Virtual Team Technology   109

Managing the Virtual Team   117

Coaching the Team You Can't See   122

Summing Up   124

8   Becoming a Team Player   127
Your Most Important Assignment

Be Open to New Ideas   129

Be Open to Different Ways of Working   130

Share What You Have   131

Seek Alternatives   132

Develop Working Relationships with People from
    Different Functions   133

Look for Win-Win Solutions   134

Only Join Teams Whose Goals You Value Highly   135

Be a Reliable Teammate   135

Be Results-Oriented   136

Summing Up   137

Appendix A: Useful Implementation Tools   139

Appendix B: A Guide to Effective Coaching   145

Appendix C: Team Troubleshooting Guide   153

Notes   155

Glossary   159

For Further Reading   161

Index   165

About the Subject Adviser   171

About the Writer   172

Creating Teams with an Edge

Introduction

The Apollo team put the first man on the moon. The first personal computers—both the Mac and the IBM—were the creations of small teams. Ford Motor Company was saved from serious decline around 1980 by Team Taurus, whose newly designed passenger car became the bestseller in North America.

Teams are responsible for many of today's accomplishments. In the business world, they have become commonplace and even fashionable—so much so that some people mistakenly believe that the team approach to attacking problems or opportunities is just another management fad. It's not. Team-based work is far from new and it's here to stay. For example, when the United States' rebellious Continental Congress decided that it needed to produce a declaration of its independence from Great Britain, it created a team to handle the job. That team included two future presidents: John Adams of Massachusetts and Thomas Jefferson, a young Virginian with wordsmithing talents. Pennsylvania's Benjamin Franklin provided some editing. Years later, when then-President Thomas Jefferson wanted to understand the half-continent he had acquired from Napoleon through the Louisiana Purchase, he didn't assign the job to a single individual, to one of his government departments, or to a unit of the regular army. Instead he gave the chore to a thirty-two-man team he called the Corps of Discovery. How that task was sponsored, staffed, organized, and led provides a useful example of what teams in any endeavor need to be successful.

As sponsor of the venture, Jefferson placed leadership in the hands of an army captain in whom he had substantial trust, a twenty-nine-

year-old Virginian named Meriwether Lewis. Jefferson did two
other things at the outset. First, he explained what he wanted: to
explore the Missouri River and whichever of its tributaries would
reach to the Pacific Ocean. Finding a water route across the uncharted regions of the northwest would be of incalculable value to
the new republic—reducing the costs and perils of shipping, and
opening the newly acquired territory to settlement. Jefferson also
wanted detailed information about the land that lay west of the Mississippi River, its flora and fauna, and its native tribes.

Second, as the team sponsor, Jefferson scraped up the money and
other resources Lewis would need to get the job done. He got the
Congress to appropriate cash over the objections of many naysayers
who condemned the venture as a hare-brained idea. Jefferson also
provided Lewis with the authority to recruit the people he needed
to complete the mission.

Having established the team's higher ends and supported it with
resources, Jefferson left the means to Lewis. In addition to assembling
the team, Lewis chose the set of skills that he would need on his
team, the specific provisions and equipment that would be carried,
and the route that the team would follow.

In picking his team, Lewis brought together people with complementary skills: frontier-hardened soldiers who had demonstrated
their resourcefulness and ability to live in the wilderness; experienced hunters whose foraging abilities would be needed to supple-
ment the provisions brought from the East; and river men familiar
with the first leg of the journey up the Missouri. Lewis also enlisted
a coleader, William Clark, whose wilderness know-how, experience
with Indians, and qualities of leadership he respected and trusted.

Lewis bolstered his own capabilities through special training. At
Jefferson's direction, he traveled to Philadelphia, where he spent
several months learning medical procedures from Dr. Benjamin
Rush. Benjamin Smith Barton, the leading natural scientist in the
Americas, taught Lewis the latest scientific methods of observing
plant and animal life, preserving specimens, and recording and clas-
sifying findings. The team leader also learned to use a sextant and

chronometer—a skill the team would require in determining and recording its position along the route.

Like many successful teams, the Corps of Discovery added and offloaded members as circumstances required. After the first leg of the journey, for example, the river men, who had little left to contribute, were sent home with scientific specimens and Lewis's progress report to Jefferson. And new capabilities were recruited as needed. Recognizing its deficiency in language skills, the team recruited a French-Canadian frontier trader named Charbonneau who lived among the Mandan tribe. Charbonneau spoke the tribe's language. Better still, his wife, Sacagawea, a Hidatsa woman, spoke the language of native people whom the Corps would encounter as it moved west.

The explorers' long trek to the Pacific coast—and back—required many on-the-spot decisions. Which branch of the river should they take? How should they deal with the tribal chieftains they encountered? Where and when should they hunker down for the long winter? Far from home and out of communication with its sponsor, the team could not defer to a higher authority but had to make its own decisions. Since the Corps was a military unit, its officers, Lewis and Clark, made most of the decisions. But other choices were put to the team as a whole. In all cases, the mission's goal guided their decisions.

The journey of the Corps of Discovery is a remarkable tale of adventure, resourcefulness, and goal-oriented struggle. As a businessperson, you are unlikely to experience anything so dramatic or challenging, yet you will surely come face-to-face with situations in which the same type of team-based approach will be the right prescription.

How prepared are you to organize and lead team-based work? Are you familiar with the characteristics of a successful team? How should a team's work fit into the work of the organization as a whole? Do you understand the role that team leaders, members, and sponsors should play in pursuing team objectives? What should you look for in recruiting team members?

These are just a few of the questions addressed in this book. Like other books in the Harvard Business Essentials series, this one is not designed to make you an expert, nor will it lead you through lengthy discourse on related academic research. Instead, it provides the advice you need to be more effective as a team sponsor, team leader, or team member.

What's Ahead

This book is organized into eight chapters. Chapter 1 explains basic concepts: how teams and traditional work groups differ, the different types of teams used by organizations, the costs and benefits of team-based work, and how you can determine whether a team is the best approach to handling a task.

If a team approach is what you need, chapter 2 can get you started. It draws on the best management literature to explain what every team must have to be successful. These qualities include competence, a clear goal, committed and contributing members, an enabling structure, a supportive organizational environment, and alignment of team goals and rewards with organizational goals.

Chapter 3 is about forming the team. It introduces the cast of characters involved in team-based work, including the sponsor, the team leader, the members, and any facilitators; the roles of these characters and how best to select them are also examined. The chapter concludes with the team charter, the formal authorization and mission given by the sponsor to the team. Lacking a clear charter, the team may not fully understand what is expected of it.

Once a team is properly formed, it needs to get off on the right foot, the subject of chapter 4. This chapter offers practical advice about the many things that must be done, and done well, if the team is to succeed. Here you'll find a discussion of the launch meeting, the importance of adopting decision rules, how to plan the work, establishing norms of team behavior, and much more.

Chances are that you are a manager or supervisor. If you are, you'll be able to use many of the skills you've already developed in your new role as a team leader—or even as a team member. There are plenty of opportunities for planning, developing and controlling a budget, motivating people, and so forth—things that you do every day. But teams also confront the manager with some unique challenges, which are taken up in chapter 5. These include the benefits of team identity and how it can be created, the perils of groupthink, and the unique roles that team leaders must play. The leader, as explained here, cannot act like a boss; doing so would neutralize the unique benefits that accrue from team-based work.

Once a team is formed and begins working toward its goals, the leader and team members need to pay attention to how it's operating. Chapter 6 examines operational issues. More specifically, this chapter explains how leaders and members can check the level of collaboration and information sharing and how they can keep people motivated. It also examines the role of learning and what can be done to assure that everyone is learning to work together effectively and that everyone is learning as quickly as possible.

Chapter 7 is about the virtual team—a team whose members are geographically dispersed. Virtual teams make it possible to bring together a more diverse group of skills and interests than would otherwise be possible. This type of team can bring together the skills of software engineers in Bombay and San Jose with a marketing whiz in San Francisco, an alliance partner in Paris, and an executive in New York. A dream team, right? Unfortunately, the benefits of virtual teams go hand-in-hand with unique management challenges. Because they rarely meet face-to-face, these teams experience more difficulty in building team identity, task collaboration, and information sharing. Such difficulties can be ameliorated through good management and the application of appropriate technologies. Chapter 7 will show you how.

Teams work best when their members and leaders behave like team players. This is not always a natural behavior. It's difficult, for example, for people to find a balance between their roles as individual performers and as team players. People accustomed to being in charge must also find ways to act like colleagues. Chapter 8 offers ideas for balancing these different roles.

These eight chapters contain the *essential* material you need to know to be an effective team leader or team member. If you'd like to dig deeper, a section entitled "For Further Reading" contains an annotated list of current books and articles on forming and managing teams.

Finally, this book contains appendixes filled with guidance on coaching team members, a number of useful worksheets and checklists, and a guide to dealing with the kinds of problems that get teams stuck. Copies of the worksheets and checklists can be downloaded from the Harvard Business Essentials series Web site, which is located at www.elearning.hbsp.org/businesstools.

The content of this book is based on a number of books, articles, and online publications of Harvard Business School Publishing—in particular, the Leading Teams module of Harvard ManageMentor®, an online service. All other sources are noted with standard endnote citations.

Team Concepts

Understand These First

Key Topics Covered in This Chapter

- *How teams and work groups differ*

- *Types of teams*

- *The costs and benefits of teams*

- *Determining whether a team is the best approach to handling a task*

T HE WORD *team* is used loosely by organizations. "We're all part of the team," a boss will tell employees. *Team* implies unity of purpose, collaboration, and, to some people, a measure of equality. Yet few human assemblages in the workplace qualify as teams. More often they are *work groups*. In a work group, each member is directed by a common manager or supervisor, but individual members do not necessarily collaborate with each other to complete their tasks. Figure 1-1 graphically illustrates the connections between members of the stereotypical work group. Here, each employee does his or her tasks as directed by the manager. Collaboration takes place between the manager and individual employees but not necessarily *between* employees. Reporting relationships are between the boss and individual employees.

Many departments and smaller units within departments operate on the work-group model. Here, each employee responds to the directives of the group leader or manager. Each employee does his or her work, often with little interaction with other unit members. In effect, the leader-manager tells each work group member, "This is our unit's goal, and this is your piece of it." If group members perform according to instruction, the goal is reached. The boss makes all the important decisions and integrates the various pieces of work, which in a team environment are crucial functions performed by the members themselves.

Work groups offer certain advantages. Coordination requirements are minimal. And assuming that (1) all the skills needed to achieve the unit's goal are represented within the group, (2) the work

FIGURE 1-1

A Work Group

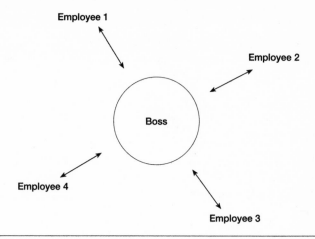

has been delegated properly, and (3) the leader-manager knows everything there is to know about achieving the common goal, everything should be fine. The traditional work group, however, has several weaknesses. It takes time for the manager to pool all the information and activity generated by group members that's needed to make decisions. Also, vesting all decision-making authority in a single person can be perilous.

In contrast to the traditional work group, a team is more than just a set of individuals who work in the same room or under the direction of a manager. A team is a small number of people with complementary skills who are committed to a common goal for which they hold themselves mutually accountable. Individual members interact with each other and with the team leader in achieving their common goal, as shown in figure 1-2. Team members depend on each other's input to perform their own work. They look to each other to complete their mission, and they look to their leader to provide resources, coaching when needed, and a link to the rest of the organization. In contrast to the work group, whose manager has decision-making authority, a team makes decisions that reflect the know-how and experience of many people; this can lead to better decisions.

FIGURE 1-2

A Team

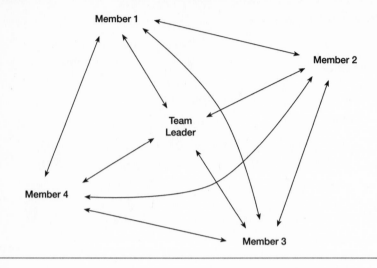

In his book *Leading Teams: Setting the Stage for Great Performances*, J. Richard Hackman concludes that real teams have four essential features: "a team task, clear boundaries, clearly specified authority to manage their own work processes, and membership stability over some reasonable period of time."[1] That is not the definition of a work group. It is important that managers understand the difference between real teams and traditional work groups, if only to avoid the common mistake of treating a traditional work group as a team, and vice versa. As Hackman observes: "If done well, either strategy can yield fine results. What is not fine is to send mixed signals: to use the rhetoric of teams when the work really is performed by individuals or to directly supervise individual members when the work really is a team's responsibility."[2]

Note: In reality, many work groups and teams do not fit the tidy definitions just offered. Instead, each has some characteristics of the other. In a practical sense, these two different types of working units operate along a continuum, with most falling somewhere between the two extremes.

Why Teams?

Organizations form different types of teams for different purposes. Here are just a few:

- Senior management teams develop philosophy, policy, and direction.

- Task forces implement specific plans for addressing problems or opportunities.

- Quality circles work on specific quality, productivity, and service problems.

- Self-managed work teams meet on a daily basis to perform an entire work process.

- Virtual teams bring geographically separate individuals together around specific tasks.

From a practical standpoint these labels and their definitions are not very important, and different organizations use them without much discipline. Two that are worth examining here, however, are self-managed work teams and project teams. They are the primary team types in use today.

Self–Managed Work Teams

A *self-managed work team* is a small group of people empowered to handle a particular ongoing task. In many cases, the team selects its leader and new members and may even have the authority to discharge members who fail to contribute or meet team standards. Consider this example:

> *Production in a steel-making minimill is organized into self-managed teams of eight employees. Each team is given base production goals, and has strong incentives to meet or exceed them. Teams have the authority to interview and hire new members as needed. Within company guidelines,*

members can also fire individual members who are unsafe, who are frequently late to work, or who otherwise impede team performance.

Members of these teams select their own leaders—often on a rotating basis—and work together on process improvement and vacation scheduling. They also determine when maintenance is required.

This type of team does essentially the same work from day to day. Its members have substantial discretion on how best to do the work, and they have incentives to establish the best procedures and to keep improving.

Project Teams

Unlike self-managed work teams, a project team is organized around a nonroutine task of limited duration. That task may take just a week or so, or it may take a year or more. When the job is done, the team disbands. Big, long-term projects with many members often have both a team leader and a full-time project manager. Consider this project-team example:

> *Phipps Corporation, a communications company with 270 employees, outgrew its office space and negotiated a lease for a larger facility several blocks away. With just ten months remaining before the move, Phipps's CEO organized a project team to handle all the details of the move. The vice president of human resources was appointed as team leader by the CEO, and she recruited representatives from all departments.*
>
> *The team had much to do. It had to develop a plan for where each department would be located in the new building. It also had to arrange for all information-technology and telephone installations, to hire a building contractor to make minor structural changes, to hire a moving company, and to work with an office-furniture company in selecting the workstation arrangements that the company required. Since the HR vice president didn't have time for day-to-day team activities, she asked a competent middle manager to spend roughly one-third of his time over the coming months to keep the project on track.*
>
> *Once the move was made, the project team terminated.*

Do You Really Need a Team?

Do you really need a team to handle a particular job? Is it the best way to achieve your goal? In most cases the answer is no. Most of the activities addressed within organizations are best handled through normal work processes or by people acting alone. For example, a sales manager has asked her salespeople to estimate the demand within their territories for a particular product. This task is not a team function; it's one that each salesperson can best handle alone. Likewise, the processing of routine loan applications at a particular bank doesn't necessarily call for a team; a well-designed work process within the loan department will do. The fact that handling loan applications is a repetitive function with few variations makes it ideal for a fast and efficient work process—and not for a team.

Teams are unnecessary when tasks are simple and routine, do not require employees to coordinate their work, and do not require a variety of experiences or skills. Teams, however, are usually the best approach when

- no individual has the right combination of knowledge, expertise, and perspective to do the job;

- individuals must work together with a high decree of interdependence; and

- the goal represents a unique challenge. (Note: A unique, infrequently occurring challenge may require a project team, but a self-managed work team often handles recurring challenges, such as meeting production quotas.)

How does your organization currently handle situations with these characteristics? If it isn't using teams, maybe it's time to think about a team approach.

Benefits and Costs

Teams have benefits and costs that differ from those of traditional work groups. When teams work well, they have many advantages:

- They can produce creative solutions.

- Group decision making produces buy-in among the people who must implement decisions.

- Teams get people in different functions to bring their separate skills to bear on intractable problems.

- Teams can enlist more information and know-how by tapping into the networks of their many members.

- They may create much better communication and collaboration within the enterprise.

Many of the advantages of teamwork flow from the synergy of the members' assembled skills and experiences. In addition, teams tend to establish new communication processes that allow for ongoing problem solving. Finally, many people enjoy team-based work. It's motivating. As a result, they deliver their best performance in a team setting.

These benefits, however, are not cost-free. Setting up a team with the right components of leadership, resources, and personnel takes time and must be managed with care and skill. Unlike a normal "set it and forget" work routine, team effort and collaboration require continual tending. There is also a greater risk that team members will fail to join together around a common goal, or that personal differences or self-interest will undermine the collaboration needed for success. Each team venture is, to some extent, an experiment whose success is not preordained.

Making the "Team Versus No-Team" Decision

As a manager, you can determine whether a team is the best solution by diagnosing the task at hand. Harvard Business School Professor Jeffrey Polzer, who has researched and written extensively on teams, urges managers to consider three aspects of a task in making this diagnosis: task complexity, task interdependence, and task objectives.[3]

1. **Task complexity.** High task complexity often lends itself to team-based work. The task features associated with high complexity include: the need to process large volumes of information; high uncertainty; many subtasks, each requiring specialized skills or knowledge; and the absence of a standardized procedure for completing the task.

2. **Task interdependence.** Here you should consider the degree of interdependence among the different components of the task. The greater the interdependence, the greater the likelihood that a team is the best solution. Polzer defines task interdependence as the extent to which features of the work itself dictate that it can only be completed by the combined efforts of multiple individuals working together. High interdependence among employees requires the exceptional coordination and communication that characterize team-based efforts. Consider this example:

   A team of engineers and industrial-design specialists have the job of developing the interior of a new minivan. Two team members specialize in automobile seats; they've devoted their entire careers to that single vehicle component. Two others specialize in ergonomics, with particular attention to the driver's situation. Three other members of the team work exclusively with materials: floor carpeting, dashboard materials, and the side and ceiling padding that absorbs road noise and provides safety in case of impact. An electrical engineer adds a very different skill set. Her job is to equip the minivan's interior with optimal lighting, sound-system outlets, and so forth. Finally, the team leader—an automotive engineer with much experience in new model design and development—completes the team. He coordinates the team's work and liaises with the chassis team, which is responsible for the structural envelope within which the minivan's interior will take shape.

   In this example, no one can do his or her job without close coordination and communication with other members of the team—and with the chassis team. The electrical engineer, for instance, could not identify the best locations for lighting and electrical features without coordinating with the ergonomics experts and the team leader. Overall, the high degree of interdependence in the work requires tight coordination between the individuals involved. These individuals rely heavily on each other in achieving the common goal. That is a key feature of team-based efforts and underscores something you must do in deciding whether a team is the best way to attack a task or problem: *Determine the degree to which distinct components of a job need to be integrated*. A high degree of integration usually requires a team effort.

3. **Task objectives.** Polzer has identified task objectives as the third critical dimension you must analyze before opting for a team or no-team approach. For a project-team effort to work, the task must have one or more clear time-bound objectives. President John F. Kennedy's challenge to NASA—to put a man on the moon and bring him home safely within ten years—fit this description. If objectives can be articulated in this way, a team effort may be the best approach. How to reach those objectives only enters the equation later. If the leader or manager cannot provide clear, time-bound objectives, then normal work routines may be more appropriate for the task.

Consider those three task dimensions, and your "team versus no-team" decision will be much better.

Summing Up

- Most organizational work is attacked through work groups or various types of teams. In a traditional work group, members are directed by a common manager or supervisor and do not necessarily collaborate with each other in completing their tasks. A team, in contrast, is a small number of individuals with complementary skills who are committed to a common goal for which they hold themselves mutually accountable. A high level of collaboration is required.

- The two primary types of teams used today are self-managed work teams and project teams. A self-managed work team is a small group of people that is empowered to handle a particular ongoing task. A project team, in contrast, is organized around a nonroutine task of limited duration. When the job is done, the team disbands.

- Teams are unnecessary when tasks are simple and routine, do not require employees to coordinate their work, and do not require a variety of experiences or skills.

- Teams are usually the best approach when no one person has the right combination of knowledge, expertise, and perspective to do the job; when individuals must work together with a high decree of interdependence; and when the goal represents a unique challenge.

- Teams have many advantages. However, they take time to organize and must be managed with care and skill.

- In making the "team versus no-team" decision, consider these three dimensions of the task in question: task complexity, task interdependence, and task objectives.

Essentials for an Effective Team

The Foundation of Success

Key Topics Covered in This Chapter

- *The importance of competence, of everyone bringing something that the team needs*

- *Why every team needs a clear goal and associated performance metrics*

- *Why commitment to the common goal is essential*

- *Why every member must contribute and every member must benefit*

- *How an enabling structure and supportive environment encourage success*

- *Why team goals must align with key organizational goals*

I F ANALYSIS of your situation confirms that a team is the best way to approach your goal, you'll probably be eager to select team members and get them into gear. Resist that impulse for just a bit. Instead, take some time to consider what your team will need to be most effective.

Management scholars and consultants have studied teams and team-based performance fairly intensely for the past twenty years. As a result, there is a large body of literature on the subject and substantial consensus on the characteristics of effective teams. This chapter examines those characteristics.

Note: The essential characteristics listed here are largely drawn from two important trains of thought on teams. Competence and commitment to a common goal reflect the work of Jon R. Katzenbach and Douglas K. Smith, whose popular book *The Wisdom of Teams: Creating the High-Performance Organization* appeared in 1993.[1] J. Richard Hackman is the source for two other key characteristics of team success: an enabling structure and supportive environment. Hackman's *Leading Teams* was published in 2002.[2] For other important ideas about teams and their management, see the list of books and articles in "For Further Reading" at the end of this book.

Competence

To succeed, the team should have all the talent, knowledge, organizational clout, experience, and technical know-how needed to get the job done. An effective team is composed of people who collectively bring all critical competencies to the effort. Any weak or missing competencies jeopardize the team goal. In these cases, teams must strengthen weaknesses or recruit for the missing competencies—something that successful teams learn to do as they move forward.

Some companies make the mistake of basing team membership on formal titles or organizational positions. Someone will suggest that "you'll really make Susan angry (or jealous) if you don't put her on your team," or that "Simon is the national sales manager, so be sure to include him on the team." Unfortunately, neither Susan's potential angst nor Simon's title is a good reason to put either of them on a team. As a team leader, your assignment is to achieve a particular goal: to design the new product line within ten months, or to reduce annual production costs by $1 million per year. Susan's frustration is not your primary consideration. Likewise, Simon may have extremely important technical and organizational competencies to contribute, but if his duties as national sales manager mean that he travels most of the time, those skills won't do your team much good. What you need are individuals who can—and will—bring critical competencies to the effort.

As a practical matter, the advice given above may need to be tempered by the political realities of the organization. For example, Susan's goodwill could be extremely important if she is in a position to block the team's progress. Making her a team member could have the effect of getting her to buy in to team objectives, thus neutralizing her danger to the team.

A Clear, Common Goal—With Performance Metrics

Have you ever been part of a team or project group that didn't have a clear idea of its purpose? If you have, you probably understand why groups like this are rarely successful. It is nearly impossible to succeed when team members cannot articulate a clear and common goal. The situation is even worse when the executives who sponsor and charter teams are unclear or uncertain about what they want done.

One way to test for a clear and common goal is to try the "elevator speech" test. Take each team member aside and ask the following question: If you were traveling by elevator between the first and second floors with our CEO and he asked what your team was working on, what would you say? Everyone on the team should be able to clearly and succinctly explain the team goal to the CEO—or to any intelligent stranger for that matter. Here are two statements that pass the elevator speech test:

- "We are redesigning our Web site with three objectives in mind: to make it capable of accommodating each of our different product groups, to make site updating and expansion faster and less costly, and to enhance the customer experience."

- "Our team is reengineering the entire customer service process. If we are successful, 95 percent of incoming customer calls will be handled by a single service rep, and 80 percent of all calls will be resolved in three minutes or less."

Can everyone on your team articulate the team goal with this degree of succinctness and clarity? Would everyone's articulation of the goal be the same? If you said no to either question, you have a problem. Try to address that problem as a group. As we explain later, a team's goal is generally handed to it by higher management, which sees a problem or opportunity and wants it dealt with. Ideally, management identifies the end but leaves the means to the team. Still, team members must share an understanding of the goal. Otherwise, they will head in different directions, dissipating both energy and resources. Conflict and bickering are guaranteed.

Once they reach a common understanding of the goal, team members, in concert with management, should specify it in terms of performance metrics. In the example of customer service reengineering, the team specified its goal as follows: "Ninety-five percent of incoming customer calls will be handled by a single service rep, and 80 percent of all calls will be resolved in three minutes or less." Metrics like these not only specify the goal more completely, they also provide a way to gauge progress toward goal completion. For example, this team could have set up interim milestones such as these:

- Within 6 months, 50 percent of incoming customer calls will be handled by a single rep.

- Within 9 months, 75 percent of incoming customer calls will be handled by a single rep.

- Within 12 months, 95 percent of incoming customer calls will be handled by a single rep.

A team without performance metrics cannot determine whether it has been successful.

Commitment to a Common Goal

A shared understanding of the goal is extremely important, but really effective teams go a step further. Their members are committed to the goal. There is a big difference between understanding and commitment. Understanding assures that people know the direction in which they should work; commitment is a visceral quality that motivates them to do the work and to keep working when the going gets tough.

Few teams have faced tougher conditions than the team of explorers led by Lewis and Clark. Every member understood the goal—to follow the Missouri River to its source and then to find a route to the Pacific Ocean. Understanding that goal was the easy part. The hard part was poling and rowing a heavy barge against the Missouri's powerful current for days on end, dealing with clouds of hungry mosquitoes in summer and subzero temperatures in winter, trekking over an unanticipated range of steep mountains, facing hostile natives and near-starvation, and finding the will to continue day after day. Most people would have turned back after the first month. Giving up would have been easy—even natural. But the members of the Corps of Discovery pressed on because they were committed to their goal, which they understood to be important to their leaders, to the president, and to the young nation that stood behind them. A deep commitment to the goal provided the energy and courage they needed to stay the course and to keep moving forward.

As that example should make clear, commitment is a function of compelling purpose. People must see their team's goal as being very important and worthy of effort. Lacking a compelling purpose, some members will not subordinate their personal goals to the team's goal. They will not identify with the team or its purpose.

Commitment is also a function of goal ownership and mutual accountability. Consider the following example:

> *A number of individuals from different functional areas of a company are brought together to solve a critical problem: Their company is losing customers to a rival that provides the same service at a markedly lower price. That lower price is a function of the rival's greater efficiency in delivering its service. The only solution is to find a way to provide customers with greater value: a lower price, measurably better service, or a combination of the two.*
>
> *Every member of the team understands the importance of the goal. Their economic futures, and those of their coworkers, depend on their success. And because management has not told team members how they should achieve their goal, they have a sense of ownership for both the effort and the result—and hold each other accountable for that result.*

That's commitment. Don't confuse shared commitment with social compatibility. It's less important that people get along with each other than it is that they are willing to work together to get things done. Having a purpose that all see as important can overcome social incompatibilities.

You can recognize shared commitment in the vocabulary used by team members. When people use *we, us,* and *our* instead of *I, you,* and *they,* team commitment is in the air. Statements like these suggest real teamwork:

- "*We* are making good progress, but each of *us* must pick up the pace."

- "Where do *we* stand with respect to *our* schedule?"

- "*Our* plan is still in the formative stages."

- "Give *us* three months and access to the customer data, and *we'll* develop a workable plan."

Commitment to a common goal is more easily achieved if the number of team members is small. That seems intuitive. The military,

Dealing with the Uncommitted but Essential Member

In an ideal world, each team member would contribute an essential skill, and each would be fully committed to the team's objective. But our world is not ideal. You may encounter this situation: An individual is assigned by a senior manager to your team because he has a unique skill without which the team is likely to fail, but you find that he is not committed to the end you seek. For example, this individual may resent being pulled away from what he sees as being more important work. How should you deal with this person, assuming that no one else in the organization has his special skill? Here are a few suggestions:

- Have a heart-to-heart talk with him in which you demonstrate how the team's goal contributes to a key goal of the company.

- Make a case for how he will benefit through team participation (see the next section).

- If all else fails, enlist the team's executive sponsor—or the individual's boss—who may be more successful than you in convincing the uncommitted team member that his job is to support the company's goal through team participation.

For advice about other team-related problems, see the "Team Troubleshooting Guide" in Appendix C.

among others, has long recognized the importance of "small group cohesion" in generating individual commitment to both the unit and its goals. Soldiers will gripe endlessly about the "damned army" but will often risk life and limb for the well-being of their infantry platoon and its individual members. For this reason, some team experts recommend membership of no more than ten individuals, and fewer is better if all the right competencies are represented.

Commitment is also enhanced through rewards. If people understand that promotions, bonuses, or pay increases are associated with their success in achieving the team goal, their commitment will increase. If they understand that the boss will get the credit and the bulk of the monetary rewards, their commitment will evaporate.

Every Member Contributes— Every Member Benefits

Have you ever been on a rowing team? If you have, you know that every member of the team must pull his or her oar with the same intensity and at the same pace as everyone else. There is no room for slackers or people who won't keep to the right pace. Work teams are very similar. Their performance depends of everyone contributing— pulling for the goal. Individual members who simply show up at meetings to render their opinions but do no work impair performance and demoralize the active teammates. If team membership has any value, it must be earned through real work. In other words, free riders—team members who obtain the benefits of membership without doing their share—cannot be tolerated.

This is not to say that every member must put in the same amount of time on team activities. A senior manager, for example, may be a regular team member even though much of his or her attention must be directed to other duties. This person may contribute by securing resources or by building support for the team within the organization. While some people might not see this contribution as real work, it is nevertheless important to the team effort.

The team leader must also do real work—including a share of the less pleasant tasks. He or she cannot be a team member *and* behave like a traditional boss, delegating all the work to others. Thus, there is a certain element of role ambiguity for the team leader, who must wear a leadership cap some of the time and a team member's cap the rest of the time. Of these roles, leading is bound to be more important, and it is indeed work.

And just as each member must contribute to the team's work, each should receive clear benefits. Benefits can take many forms: the emotional/psychological reward of doing interesting and meaningful work, a learning experience that will pay future career dividends, or extra money in a paycheck. In the absence of clear benefits, individuals will not contribute at a high level—at least not for long; the benefits they derive from their regular jobs will absorb their attention and make team duties a secondary priority.

A Supportive Environment

No business team operates in a vacuum. A team is a small organization embedded within a larger environment of operating units and functional departments. It depends on its organizational kin to one degree or another for resources, information, and assistance. The extent to which operating units and departments are supportive, indifferent, or hostile to the team and it goals is bound to have an impact on team effectiveness. In particular, the team builder needs to consider these environmental factors:

- **Leadership support.** Support at the top is essential. It ensures resources and helps recruit the right people. Leadership support also provides protection from powerful managers and departments that for one reason or another would be inclined to torpedo the team effort.

- **A nonhierarchical structure.** Team-based work is more likely to be successful if the organization does not conform to a rigid hierarchical structure. Why? Because a nonhierarchical structure creates habits that are conducive to team-based work: specifically, a willingness to share information, collaboration across organizational boundaries, and employee empowerment. These habits are weak or absent in organizations where the bosses do all the thinking and directing and everyone else follows orders. Such organizations are not team-ready.

- **Appropriate reward systems.** Companies that are new to team-based work need to examine their reward systems before launching teams; they must find a different balance in rewards for individual and team-based success. Doing so is one of the most daunting challenges faced by those who sponsor teams.

- **Experience with team-based work.** Teams benefit when their companies and individual members have plenty of experience with team-based work. Experience provides insights into what works and what does not, how best to organize around a goal, how to collaborate, and how to alter the team at different points in its life cycle. Many companies that rely on team-based work provide training on team methods, and with good reason. Individuals must be trained in team-based work. Specifically, they need help with skills such as listening, communicating with different kinds of people, collaborating with people outside their departments, and staying focused on the common task.

How supportive of team-based work is your organization? Is it prepared (through training or experience) to attack problems or opportunities using teams?

Alignment

Alignment is the last item on our list of essentials for team effectiveness. Alignment refers to the coordination of plans, effort, and rewards with an organization's highest goals. In an aligned organization, everyone understands both the goals of the enterprise and the goals of his or her operating unit. In an aligned organization people work in the right direction—and the rewards system encourages them to do so.

Teams also need alignment. A team shouldn't even exist unless it represents the best way to help the organization achieve its goals. So team goals should align with organizational goals, and the goals of individual team members should align—through the team—with those higher organizational goals. And everyone's efforts should align through the rewards system. This last point is very important, and it begins at the top, with the sponsor. Since the sponsor is accountable for team success, some part of his or her compensation should be linked to the team's performance. Moving down the line, the team's leader and members should likewise see their compensation affected by team outcomes. Figure 2-1 illustrates the integrated levels of work, goal, and reward alignment.

Alignment gets everyone moving in the same direction—the right direction.

FIGURE 2-1

Team Alignment

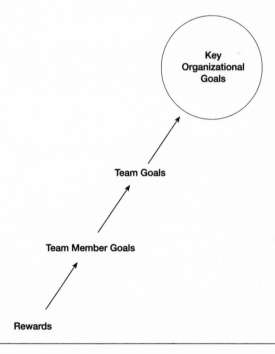

Summing Up

- Competence is a prime ingredient of team effectiveness. An effective team is composed of people who collectively bring all critical competencies to the effort. Missing competencies must either be recruited or developed internally.

- Commitment to the goal is another essential ingredient of team success. You can assure commitment by directing teams toward compelling goals and things that really matter to the organization, keeping teams at no more than ten members, and aligning team-based work with tangible rewards.

- Every member should contribute and every member should receive benefits.

- Make sure that the organization's structure is compatible with team-based work, and that it encourages success.

- Align team goals with organizational goals.

3

Forming the Team

The Crew and Its Charter

Key Topics Covered in This Chapter

- *Sponsor, leaders, and their functions*

- *Selecting team members*

- *The importance of a team charter*

T EAMS ARE FORMED in various ways. In many cases, individuals working on a common problem will organize themselves. In other cases, an executive or manager will organize a team around a perceived need. Consider this example:

As board chairman of a community-development organization, Mel was unhappy with the quality and consistency of the periodic press releases and newspaper reports that described the organization's activities and views. Up to that time, individual board members and the program director had written letters to the editor of the local paper or submitted press releases to communicate their opinions or group activities. The results were as haphazard as the approach. Mel knew that a consistent and unified communications strategy was needed. "To be successful as an organization," he told the board, "we have to inform the local business community, potential volunteers, and potential contributors about our mission and what we are doing to improve the local economy. In my view, that translates into a monthly newsletter, professional-quality press releases, announcements about events, and newspaper editorials that address our issues." Board members nodded in agreement.

At Mel's urging, several people volunteered to form a communications team. Together, the team's membership represented the organization's staff and different shades of board opinion. These individuals agreed to meet, form a team, select a leader, and develop and execute a communications strategy.

Mel liked the idea and appreciated their initiative. "And if you are agreeable," he told them, "I will ask my friend Helen LaTour if she'd be willing to provide some help. She has had plenty of newspaper

experience, and she has developed newsletters for a variety of organiza-
tions." The volunteer team members agreed that Helen could facilitate
their effort. "We'll begin meeting next week," said one of them, "and
we'll report back to the board next month with a communications
strategy."

This example illustrates how some teams are formed and the typical
cast of characters involved, which include a sponsor (Mel), a team
leader (to be determined), members (the volunteers), and, in some
cases, a facilitator (Helen). Let's examine this cast of characters in
greater detail.

Team Sponsor

Whether a team is formed by a manager or by a group of staff members, a team must have a sponsor. As Michael Wachter has described
in *8 Lies of Teamwork,* "No team should be formed without an executive sponsor committed to its success."[1] That sponsor should be a
manager or executive who has a real stake in the outcome and who
is accountable for the team's performance. The sponsor should also
have the authority to define the scope of the work, provide necessary
resources, and approve or reject team output. In the example that
opened this chapter, the sponsor recognized the importance of the
team's task. Mel acknowledged the importance of a consistent and
unified strategy for communicating with stakeholders and the public. As the organization's chairman, he had a clear interest in the results produced by the team and in its strategy, and he had the
authority to define the scope of the communications team's work
and pass judgment on it.

In large organizations, the sponsor also acts as patron, provider of
resources, protector against internal saboteurs, and encourager. The
authors of a book on radical innovation projects observed in each of
the ten cases they studied that a highly placed sponsor, or patron, was
instrumental in providing these critical services.[2] Sponsors kept projects alive by providing funding—sometimes through normal channels, and sometimes under the table—by fending off attempts to

terminate them, and by promoting the value of project goals to higher management.

The sponsor should champion the team's goals at the highest level, reminding the leadership of how the team's success will contribute to the organization's success. Alignment of the team's goals with organizational goals makes this job easier. And, as implied earlier, the sponsor must shield the team from high-level enemies who see its activities as a threat to their personal turf. That protection is particularly critical when a team is working to develop products or technologies that, if successful, will cannibalize sales from current products or render them obsolete. In such instances, powerful executives who represent the current product lines are likely to be hostile to the team's goals and may use their power to withhold funding or discredit the team's work. Here it is wise to recall Machiavelli's warning to all who attempt to alter the status quo: "There is nothing more difficult to carry out, or more doubtful of success, nor more dangerous to handle, than to initiate a new order of things. For the reformer has enemies in all those who profit from the old order."[3]

Does your team have an influential sponsor? If it does, is this sponsor acting as a true champion by providing resources and fending off internal naysayers?

Team Sponsor's To-Do List

- Ensure that the team's progress is communicated to the rest of the organization and, in particular, to the leadership.

- Ensure that senior management supports the team's decisions and direction.

- Be alert to any change in company objectives that may affect the team's charter.

- Remember that some managers will not want their subordinates to split their time between team duties and regular assignments. Work with these managers to smooth over difficulties.

If you are a senior executive, think about the people you put forward as team sponsors. Are they really committed to their teams' success? Do they act as team champions, or do they simply go through the motions? Have you arranged things so that they have a personal stake in the teams' success or failure?

Team Leader

Every team needs a leader. In many respects, the job of the team leader is similar to that of the traditional manager. Both are charged with obtaining results through people and other resources. And like the traditional manager, the team leader must also do the following: provide a framework for the team's activities, keep the vision clear, coordinate activities, represent the team to others, negotiate with the sponsor, mediate conflicts, identify needed resources, set milestones, ensure that everyone contributes and benefits, and keep work on track. Don't they sound like the typical manager's duties?

But this is where the similarity ends. Traditional managers take on the roles of decision maker, delegator, director, and scheduler of others' work. These roles don't work well within teams. The team leader cannot act like the boss and still obtain the benefits of the team. Instead, a team leader adopts three new roles: initiator, model, and coach. He or she must also pitch in as a working member.

What are the characteristics of a person who can do most, or all, of these things? For starters, the team leader should have traditional leadership skills: the ability to set a direction that others will follow, good communication skills, the ability to give and accept feedback, and high standards for performance. Beyond those, the potential team leader should have a positive attitude toward team-based work—and preferably have experience with it. The last person you'd want to fill the job would be someone who insists on acting like a traditional boss.

Choosing the Leader

The sponsor may assign a team leader if the team will be short-lived, if there is an immediate need for a team (as in a crisis situation), or if there is an organizational reason for a certain person to be team leader. In other circumstances, the team may select its own leader.

One Leader or Several?

We generally think that a single formal leader is required for any particular unit. Investing leadership in a single person assures that authority has an undivided voice. How, after all, would a team get things done if it had two bickering leaders? Whose direction would people follow?

The experience of teams indicates that investing leadership in a single person is not an absolute necessity as long as there is agreement among leaders on means and ends. The success of Meriwether Lewis and his hand-picked coleader, William Clark, in leading the Corps of Discovery across the uncharted wilderness west of the Mississippi River testifies to the potential value of investing leadership in two or more persons. Both men had served together in the regular army (Clark was Lewis's commanding officer) and enjoyed mutual trust and respect. And each brought important complementary skills to the venture. As described by historian Bernard DeVoto:

> Lewis was the diplomatic and commercial thinker, Clark the negotiator. Lewis, who went specially to Philadelphia for training in botany, zoology, and celestial navigation, was the scientific specialist; Clark the engineer and geographer as well as master of frontier crafts. Both were experienced rivermen but Lewis acknowledged that Clark had greater skill and usually left the management of the boats to him. Clark evidently had the greater gift for dealing with Indians.[4]

Their temperaments were likewise complimentary. Per DeVoto, Lewis was mercurial and introverted, whereas his coleader was even tempered and extroverted. What one man lacked, the other supplied.

Not every team will benefit from multiple leaders, but some will. Just be sure that the leaders are of one mind as to their goal and its importance.

By virtue of his or her appointment, the team leader enjoys formal authority. But a team also needs leadership within the ranks and

Team Leader's To-Do List

- Regularly communicate progress and problems with the sponsor.

- Periodically assess team progress, the outlook of members, and how each member views his or her contribution.

- Make sure that everyone contributes and everyone's voice is heard.

- Do a share of the work.

- Resist the urge to act like a boss.

at different levels. For example, several team members may be assigned to develop and test a new product prototype. Leadership is required within this "team within the team" to coordinate the effort, communicate with others, and secure necessary resources. Whoever acts as the leader of this ad hoc group will have no formal authority but will be required to do what leaders do.

Team Members

The heart of any team, and the true engine of its work, is its membership. Yes, a good sponsor can clear the way and secure resources, and, yes, a good leader can motivate performance and keep work focused. But it's the team members who do most of the work. As a consequence, bringing together the right people with the right skills is extremely important.

When Lewis and Clark selected members of the Corps of Discovery, they had no shortage of volunteers. But they were smart in accepting only those who had something important to contribute. Many young gentlemen with good connections were put forward as candidates, but all were rejected. Even Benjamin Smith Barton,

Lewis's tutor in biology and one of the most eminent natural scientists of his day, failed to make the cut. Barton's knowledge would have contributed greatly to one aspect of the mission—cataloging the flora and fauna of the undiscovered American West. But Lewis thought Barton, who was thirty-seven years old, was unfit for the rigors of the journey that lay ahead.

In selecting their team, the two coleaders enlisted men with an eye toward physical toughness, character, and skills. As described by the late historian Stephen Ambrose: "Lewis and Clark sized them up, making judgments on their general hardiness, their shooting and hunting ability, their physical strength and general character, their suitability for a long journey in the wilderness."[5] And the leaders' high standards for selection paid off.

According to experts, choosing good team members is probably the trickiest part of designing a team. A team can acquire its members in one or more of the following ways:

- **Assignment.** The sponsor selects the people and invites them to participate.

- **Voluntary.** The people most invested or most interested in the work step forward as potential members.

- **Nomination.** People who have an interest in the project nominate individuals who have the right skills and in whom they have confidence.

None of those selection methods is inherently better or worse than the others. Each is capable of tapping the right members. But each is equally capable of putting the wrong people on a team, particularly when the organization is highly politicized. Consider these examples:

- The sponsor has selected most of the members of a new Web site design team. Among them is Hugh, the sponsor's right-hand man. Hugh doesn't know a server from a hyperlink and has nothing in particular to contribute to the team effort. His only purpose will be to report back to the sponsor, who distrusts two team members. For the team, Hugh is excess baggage. Other team members will quickly discover his role as informant and will react negatively.

- Ann has volunteered for a team that's being organized to reengineer the company's order-fulfillment process. Ann isn't particularly interested in the team's objective, but she sees membership as a way to get face time with Katherine, the team leader and a rising manager in the company. Ann is also concerned that her main rival for a promotion is already on the team. "If he's on that team, I had better be on it too," she reasons. It's clear that Ann's commitment is not to the team's objective but to her own self-interest. As a consequence, she should not be enlisted.

- Harry has volunteered for the same reengineering team. He has a proprietary interest in the current order-fulfillment process and believes that his organizational standing will suffer if the team adopts a radical makeover of that process. His motivation is self-protection. Harry's commitment is not to the team's objective but to the status quo. He absolutely should not be on the team.

- Ralph has nominated Muriel, one of his direct reports, to the Web site design team. "This will be a good learning experience for her" he tells himself. Yes, Muriel's participation might be a very good thing for her career development, but will it be a very good thing for the team? What does she have to contribute?

Do you see examples like these in your organization? If you do, watch out. In each scenario, an individual was put forward as a team member for a reason that had nothing to do with helping the team achieve its stated goals. Such approaches to team selection should be avoided. A case might be made for Muriel's inclusion in the team, however, if she was a fast learner and a hard worker. But the achievement of team goals must have priority over the development of individual members.

Skill assessment

Team selection should ideally be determined by the skills needed to accomplish the work. Consider this example, as described by Gregory Watson in his book *Strategic Benchmarking*:

> *Back in the late 1970s, Ford Motor Company's top management opted to bet the company on a new, built from scratch, car model that would become known as the Taurus. Every functional group in the company would be involved, as usual. But this time the job would not be attacked through the usual over-the-wall approach, but through a cross-functional team headed by a senior project manager named Lew Veraldi. Veraldi had broad discretion in selecting team members, which he accomplished by mapping all required areas of technical and market expertise needed to produce and launch a new car model. Team membership was represented through two levels: an inner circle of key people numbering less than ten, and a larger set of players numbering over 400. It would take that many to get the job done. Only a fraction of these would dedicate 100 percent of their time to Team Taurus work. Each team member, however, would bring along all the know-how and resources of his or her functional department.* [6]

Skill assessment is a two-stage process: The first stage looks objectively at the job and determines exactly what skills are needed to get it done. This is essentially what Veraldi did with his mapping exercise. For example, he recruited people from component engineering, manufacturing, parts and service, purchasing, legal, and sales and marketing. Together, they represented all the skills and resources needed to produce and sell the new automobile under development.

The second stage of skill assessment looks at the people in the organization and determines which have the right skills. Teams must be composed of members who collectively bring all the necessary skills—whether technical, problem-solving, interpersonal, or organizational—to the job.

- **Technical skill** refers to specific expertise—in market research, finance, software programming, and so forth.

- **Problem–solving skill** is an individual's ability to analyze difficult situations or impasses and to craft solutions. Engineers are trained as problem solvers. Creative people have habits of mind that help them see resolutions that others may not see. If you're the leader, you need problem solvers on your team; otherwise, people will continually look to you for solutions—and that is not a teamwise approach.

- **Interpersonal skill** refers to an ability to work effectively with others—a very important trait for team-based work.

- **Organizational skills** include the ability to communicate with other units, knowledge of the company's political landscape, and possession of a network. People with these skills help the team get things done and avoid conflict with operating units and their personnel.

Those who form the team must look closely at the results they expect from it and must determine the various activities that will produce those results. Then they must ask themselves what skills those activities require.

When forming teams, managers have a natural tendency to limit their task analysis to technical skills. It's so obvious that specific technical capabilities are needed that team builders focus on them to the exclusion of other skills. As Jeffrey Polzer writes: "This is a sensible starting point because, for example, a software development team cannot work very well without programmers who know the particular coding language to be used in the project; nor can an orchestra succeed without individually talented musicians."[7] Unfortunately, attention to technical skills often overshadows attention to interpersonal and organizational skills, which in the long run may be just as important. For instance, a brilliant programmer may actually retard team progress if she is secretive about her work, is unwilling to collaborate, or generates hostility among other members. On the same note, a person with average technical skills but superb organizational savvy could be the team's most valuable member, thanks to her ability to gather resources, enlist help from operating units, and so forth.

Edison's Insomnia Brigade

Few teams have made as many and as significant breakthroughs as the one formed by Thomas Edison. Dubbed the "Insomnia Brigade" because of its leader's ability to press through the day and night with about four hours of sleep and catnaps, the Edison invention team obtained hundreds of patents and introduced dozens of important products during the final decades of the nineteenth century.

The origins of the Insomnia Brigade can be traced to Edison's initial thinking about the prospect of producing the incandescent electric lamp, which he saw as a huge commercial opportunity. Knowing that he would have to do lots of experimenting with designs and materials, he carefully created a team that included technicians with machining, laboratory, and glassblowing skills. Their skills made it possible for him to test hundreds of filament materials in rapid succession. Eventually, a vacuum bulb containing a carbonized cotton filament proved serviceable. But more experiments with materials were needed before Edison's idea could be commercialized. The technical skill set he assembled made that possible and put him ahead of other inventors who were attempting to do the same thing.

Polzer cautions that there is plenty of room for the talented individual contributor who isn't very good at working with others, concluding that a person's interpersonal weaknesses may be addressed through coaching or other means. This advice should encourage managers to be sanguine about the positive and negative characteristics of potential team members. Individuals who are strong on all four measures—technical, problem-solving, interpersonal, and organizational—are few and far between. Thus, one of the goals of member selection must be to make the most of the available talent and take steps to neutralize people's weaknesses.

Most experts on team creation caution that you'll rarely get all the skills you need on the team. Something will always be missing.

And in most cases, it is impossible to anticipate every skill needed. As Jon Katzenbach and Douglas Smith have note: "No team succeeds without all the skills needed to meet its purpose and performance goals. Yet most teams figure out the skill they will need *after* [our emphasis] they are formed."[8] Thus, the savvy team leader looks for people with both valued skills and the potential to learn new ones as needed.

Adding and Subtracting Members

Be prepared to add new members and possibly bid thanks and good-bye to others over time. New skills and members may be needed as the work changes and the team makes progress toward its goal. Consider the example of a process-reengineering team that was charged with redesigning a company's entire customer service function. This team began as a small core group of five members. Over the first year of its life, it recruited five additional members—each representing one of the company's product groups. Once this team completed the plan for customer service redesign, it moved to an implementation stage. At that point, still more people were recruited—people who would play major roles in plan implementation.

One caution on adding and offloading members: Over time, members adjust to the people and working styles represented within the team. They develop effective patterns for making decisions and communicating—and sometimes do so very gradually. They identify the team with the other players. This cohesion is undermined when too many people join and exit the team. Those who remain must spend lots of valuable time orienting the new members and learning how to work with them; they must spend still more time finding ways to fill in for departed team members. So minimize turnover as much as possible.

Once a candidate for membership has been identified, his or her potential contribution should be discussed by the team and with the sponsor. The candidate's supervisor should also be consulted, as team membership absorbs time that the candidate would otherwise spend on regular assignments. Assuming agreement among all parties, the candidate can then be invited to join.

How Many Is Too Many?

The optimal size for a team depends on its goals and tasks. In general, small teams of five to ten members tend to be most effective when the tasks are complex and require specific skills. Larger teams (up to twenty-five people) can be effective if their tasks are fairly simple and straightforward and team members agree to delegate tasks to subgroups as needed. Including an odd number of people on the team can facilitate decision making, since majority-rules votes never end in ties.

The best advice about how many people to have on a team is this: Have just enough people to do the job and no more. Having too few people will slow you down and possibly mean that you don't have all the requisite skills. Having too many will also slow you down by shifting valuable time and energy into communication and coordination efforts. There is also the problem of commitment. Individual commitment to the team and its goals tends to diminish as more people are added

Authors Jon Katzenbach and Douglas Smith offer these cues to knowing whether your team is small enough:[9]

- The team can convene easily and frequently.

- Members can communicate easily and frequently.

- No additional people are required to get the job done.

Team Members' To-Do List

- Complete all assigned tasks on time.

- Communicate dissatisfactions and concerns with the leader and other members.

- Support the leader and other members.

- Help others when they need help, and ask for help when you need it.

Facilitator

The last potential actor in the cast of team characters is a *facilitator*. We use the term *potential* because, unlike all other participants, facilitators aren't always necessary. They are there to help—but only when help is really needed.

Facilitators are generally either outside consultants or human resources personnel with special training in team-based work. Unlike other team members, they do not involve themselves with team tasks. Instead, they either provide expert technical advice or help optimize collaboration and communication. In our initial example, Mel had Helen, a person with substantial communications experience, help the new communications committee develop its strategy. More typically, a facilitator will observe team interactions as a neutral third party and speak up when he or she sees progress-sapping conflicts, the absence of clear priorities, or opportunities for greater collaboration.

Many large companies for which teams are a regular function use facilitators to conduct teamwork training. Employees who have had no experience with team-based work are sent to a two- or three-day workshop led by the facilitator-trainers.

Note: Appendix A at the end of this book contains two items that can help you as you form your team: "Worksheet for Forming a Team" and "Checklist for Evaluating Whether a Group Is a Team." You can obtain free downloadable copies of these items from the Harvard Business Essentials Web site, which is located at www.elearning.hbsp.org/businesstools.

The Team Charter

Having the right cast of characters is important. But so is having a *charter* that spells out the nature of the work and senior management's expectations for results. Without a formal charter, the team can head off in a direction that is not aligned with organizational objectives. And creating a charter forces senior management to clearly articulate what the team should do—an important step when the organization's leaders are not of one mind, as in this example:

Phil was the sponsor of the company's effort to reengineer its order-fulfillment and customer service operations. As an outspoken critic of these functions, he was the right person for the job. He had long been dissatisfied with the time it took to fill orders and with the company's unspectacular level of customer service. In addition, he thought the costs of these operations were too high. So he put Lila in charge of a team effort to improve them.

What sorts of cost cutting was Phil anticipating? What exactly were his complaints about the current system? What would success look like? Lila attempted to pin Phil down on those questions, but without success. He was too busy to think it all through and too eager to delegate responsibility for the team's outcome. Other company executives were also anxious to see improvements but, like Phil, had no clear ideas about the outcomes they wanted. So when Lila sounded out senior managers about the subject, they cited no specific goals. Lacking clear guidance, Lila and the people on the team developed their own goals and criteria for success.

The team pushed forward, and Lila reported progress to Phil over the course of the effort. Resources were always a problem, particularly since Lila was never sure how much money she could spend and how many people she could bring on to the team at key stages. Every request for resources had to be negotiated on a case-by-case basis with Phil.

The team eventually completed its tasks, meeting all of its self-declared goals. It had cut order-fulfillment time by one-third. Ninety percent of customers could now get all their issues resolved with a single phone call. And the overall cost of these functions had been cut by 12 percent. The team celebrated the completion of its duties with a splendid dinner, after which its members went back to their regular duties.

Senior management, however, was not entirely pleased with the outcome. "You did a pretty good job," Phil told Lila. "The improvements you've made are significant, but we were looking for a more sweeping reorganization and larger cost savings." Lila was stunned and more than slightly angry. "If he wanted these things," she thought, "why didn't he say so?"

Situations like Lila's are common, but can be avoided through a team charter. A team charter is a concise written document containing some or all of the following:

- Name of project sponsor

- Relationship and priority of the team's work to unit or corporate goals

- Expected time frame of the work

- Concise description of project deliverables

- The project's benefits

- The budget, allocations, and resources available to the team

- The team's authority

- The sponsor's signature

A thoughtful charter indicates the end but does not specify the means. The means should be left to the team leader and members. Doing otherwise—that is, telling the team what it should do *and* how to do it—would undermine any benefit derived from a team effort. Richard Hackman makes this clear in his book *Leading Teams*. "Direction that is unclear or extremely abstract," he writes, "can waste members' time and embroil them in conflicts as they struggle to agree on what they are really supposed to do. Direction that is *too* clear and complete, on the other hand, can lessen members' commitment to the work and sometimes prompt unwanted and even unethical behaviors." As he sees it, the sponsor must find a balance between giving the team too much and too little specific direction.[10]

As Hackman makes clear in figure 3-1, teams do best when the ends are specified and the means are not (upper-right quadrant), when they do goal-oriented work and manage themselves. As he writes: "When ends are specified but means are not, team members are able to—indeed, are implicitly encouraged to—draw on their full complement of knowledge, skill, and experience in devising and executing a way of operating that is well tuned to the team's purpose and

FIGURE 3-1

Means and Ends

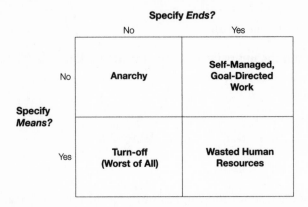

Source: J. Richard Hackman, *Leading Teams: Setting the Stage for Great Performances* (Boston: Harvard Business School Press, 2002), 73. Reproduced with permission.

circumstances."[11] This is not to say that specifying *both* ends and means (lower-right quadrant) will necessarily lead to failure. But that situation more closely describes a traditional, unempowered work group.

Once the charter is established and the team organized, the team can develop its own specification of the means by creating a *project plan*. With the sponsor's approval, this plan becomes part two of the charter.

A project plan is especially useful for large, complex endeavors. It provides more detail about tasks, milestones, deliverables, risks, and timetables. The project plan serves as a road map, both for the team and other interested parties.

Aligning Behavior Through Rewards

The final part of the team-forming process discussed in this chapter is creating incentives. If people do not see rewards or incentives for achieving team goals, they are unlikely to give those goals the attention they require. Instead, their attention will be drawn elsewhere, most likely to their regular jobs, which are rewarded with job-based pay, the prospect of promotion, and, in many cases, performance-based bonuses. Such incentives are designed to align the employees' efforts with the organization's higher goals. Something must be done to align efforts with the team's goals, which raises a number of knotty questions:

- How can the reward system be altered to address the fact that team members may be spending X percent of their time on traditional work done to advance their unit goals and Y percent on team-based work, which serves other goals?

- Teamwork requires high levels of interdependent work and mutual accountability for results. So, should rewards be based on individual contributions to team goals or on the performance of the team as a whole?

- If team-based rewards are used, how can free riding—that is, rewarding of noncontributing members—be avoided? The hardworking members of the team will be demoralized if they know that others are riding their coattails to substantial rewards.

The business of team rewards is very complex. For one thing, the organization already has a rewards system in place that has nothing to do with the team. It will not want to alter that system. Furthermore, the tension between using team rewards and discouraging free riding has a long history. There are no easy answers. In general, the best approach is to use team rewards coupled with mechanisms that discourage free riding. The most obvious of these mechanisms is to keep free riders off teams in the first place. If one or two slip through the member-recruiting process, the leader and members should thank them for their contributions and send them back to their regular duties.

Summing Up

- Every team should have a sponsor committed to its success. That sponsor should be a manager or executive who has a real stake in the outcome and who is accountable for the team's performance. The sponsor should also have the authority to define the scope of the work, provide it with necessary resources, and approve or reject team output.

- A team leader must fulfill many of the responsibilities of the traditional manager. In addition, he or she must adopt three new roles: initiator, model, and coach.

- Selection of team members should be determined by the skills needed to accomplish the work. First, analyze the goal to determine what technical, problem-solving, interpersonal, and organizational skills are needed to achieve it; then identify and recruit people who have those skills.

- In forming a team, recruit as many people as you need to get the job done—but no more.

- A team charter spells out the nature of the work and management's expectations for results. It points team efforts in a direction that is aligned with organizational objectives. Writing the charter forces senior management to clearly articulate what the team should do.

- Use rewards to align team members' interests with the organization's goals.

4

Getting Off on the Right Foot

Important First Steps

Key Topics Covered in This Chapter

- *Hosting a launch meeting*

- *Adopting decision rules*

- *Planning and scheduling the work*

- *Agreeing on measures of success*

- *Developing a budget*

- *Setting up mechanisms that hold the team together*

- *Laying down norms of behavior*

ONCE A TEAM has been formed and its charter delivered, several important things must be done before work commences. Rules must be established about the *who* and *how* of decisions, and also about how members will behave toward each other. Plans must be made for achieving team goals. The work must be broken down into manageable pieces, scheduled for completion, and allocated to the right people. These are just a few of the issues that the team must address at the very beginning of the team effort. Together, they create a framework within which effective team work can be done. Some of the important issues can be addressed in an initial team meeting.

Host a Launch Meeting

The best way to launch a team effort is through an all-team meeting, one with appropriate levels of gravity and fanfare. Much discussion and planning will obviously have been undertaken prior to the launch meeting, often between the team leader or sponsor and the individual members. But those informal get-togethers are no substitute for a face-to-face meeting attended by all members, the team leader, the sponsor, and, if appropriate, the highest-ranking official of the organization.

Physical presence at this meeting has great psychological importance, particularly for geographically dispersed teams, whose members may have few future opportunities to convene as a group. Being to-gether at the very start of their long journey and getting to know each other at a personal level will help build commitment and bol-ster participants' sense that this team and project are important. It's hard to imagine anyone getting a sense of being part of a group with common goals without being in the physical presence of his or her teammates at some point. If certain people cannot attend the launch meeting because of their geographic location, every effort should be made to give them a virtual presence through videoconferencing or, at the very least, speakerphone. Yes, lots of teams these days don't have the benefit of being in one another's physical presence, but some nevertheless succeed in fostering team identity and common goals. Despite the success stories, not being colocated is a handicap—one that should be avoided if possible.

The sponsor's presence at the launch meeting is also imperative, and his or her demeanor will speak volumes about the importance—or unimportance—ascribed to the team's mission. As experts Jon Katzenbach and Douglas Smith write:

> *When potential teams first gather, everyone monitors the signals given by others to confirm, suspend, or dispel assumptions and concerns. They pay particular attention to those in authority: the team leader and any executives who set up, oversee, or otherwise influence the team. And, as always, what such leaders do is more important than what they say. If a senior executive leaves the team kickoff to take a phone call ten min-utes after the session has begun and he never returns, people get the message.*[1]

Here are things you should aim to accomplish at the launch meeting:

- Be very clear on who belongs to the team. There may be core members, and there may be peripheral members who partici-pate for a limited time or in a limited capacity. Both are mem-bers. Do not tolerate any ambiguity on this point. Welcome all who belong to the team to the launch meeting.

- Explain the charter and its contents. The sponsor or team leader should explain the goal, deliverables, timetables, and so forth in the charter.

- Seek unanimous understanding of the charter. Just because the leadership explains the goal, deliverables, and so on is no assurance that every team member will interpret the remarks in the same way. Engage people in discussion about the charter with the goal of getting agreement and consensus.

- The sponsor should explain why the team's work is important and how its goals fit with larger organizational objectives. People need to know that they are part of something with important consequences for themselves and the organization.

- Describe the resources available to the team and the nonteam personnel with whom members are likely to interact. That group may include company employees, employees of alliance partners, suppliers, or customers.

- Describe the team incentives. What, besides their normal compensation, will members receive if team goals are met or exceeded?

- Make introductions. Unless people are already familiar with each other and their work, use the launch meeting as an opportunity for that purpose. If the group is of a reasonable size, ask participants to introduce themselves, say something about their background and expertise, and explain what they hope to contribute to the effort.

By the end of the launch meeting, people should have a clear sense of direction, the importance of the team goal to the organization, how success will be measured, and how they will be rewarded for their efforts. They should know who's on the team and what each is capable of contributing. And they should begin to think of themselves as a real team. A true sense of teamship can only develop with time and through shared experiences. Nevertheless, the seeds should be planted at the launch meeting.

Decide About Decisions

Very early on, the team must agree on how decisions will be made. If it lacks consensus, the team will either waste a lot of time or produce decisions that many will not support. And decisions are waiting around every corner:

Should one minor goal be traded off for another?

Three alternative new product designs are on the table. Which will the team select?

Which consultant should the team hire, and how should the scope of the consulting engagement be defined?

The team is overspending its budget: Which activities should be cut?

In nonteam environments, decisions are the domain of executives and managers. These individuals identify the issue, seek out and analyze alternatives, and take counsel from appropriate sources. They then make a decision and accept responsibility for the consequences. Decision making within their own scope of responsibility is one of the things that managers and executives are paid to do. Though they may seek consensus and the input of others, they are not bound by others' opinions.

Team decision making is not so clear-cut. Sponsors obviously have decision-making authority over team goals and the level of resources allocated to the team. They also maintain ultimate authority on

- personnel;

- expenditures over a given budget amount;

- bringing in outside resources;

- changes in organizationwide policy or goals;

- choices affecting customers, such as pricing and specifications; and

- changes in the team's deliverables and schedule.

Decision Procedures Matter

Research indicates that people really care about decision procedures. They want protocol to be fair, and they are much more likely to accept a decision that is unfavorable to them as long as they believe the procedure for making the decision was fair. Trust is a key element in this situation. People must trust those who devise the decision-making procedure. If they see others rigging it and acting out of self-interest, then their willingness to accept decisions will evaporate.

Teams, on the other hand, should have sole authority over decisions related to team operations and processes. In addition, they may make resource decisions within a specified budget limit. To avoid potential disagreements, be sure that your team, its sponsor, and higher management have a shared understanding of which decisions the team can make and which will be made outside the group.

If you are a team leader, one of the things you must do to get the team started is to help it agree on the *who* and *how* of decision making. Who will make the decisions? Will it be the team leader or a subset of individuals, or will all members have a say? How will decisions be made? Will the majority rule? Must the group reach full consensus of opinion? Will decisions be final? If not, what kind of modification process will it follow?

Here are some common decision-making approaches:

- **Majority rule.** Team members bring input to the meeting, discuss, and then vote. The decision that receives more than 50 percent of the votes is adopted.

- **Consensus.** Every member of the team must agree to adopt a decision. If consensus cannot be reached, new alternatives must be developed and brought back to the group.

- **Small group decides.** A group of individuals with relevant experience and skills is selected to make decisions.

- **Leader decides with input.** The team leader gathers input from team members and then makes the decision.

In selecting a decision-making approach, a team should weigh the trade-offs. The more involved the team members are in the decision-making process, the more likely it is that they will support the outcome. As a result, the consensus and majority-rules approaches can help build team commitment. Those approaches, however, take time—something the team may or may not have built into its schedule. If time is an issue, the team might consider using different approaches for different types of decisions: It could reach an agreement collectively on issues that are most important to members and use a more streamlined approach for the rest.

Whichever choices are made about decision making, establishing them during the team's start-up stage is extremely important. Failing to lay out the decision rules will lead to bickering and dissension. If time and events indicate that those rules are not supporting key goals, change them in an orderly manner.

A Caution on Consensus

It's easy to confuse consensus about an issue with unanimous support. The two are not always the same. Consultant Michael Wachter makes the point that what often appears to be consensus is simply the outcome of some people voting in favor just to end a deadlock and move on. That does not represent real support for the decision. In other cases, some members may, like politicians, agree to a decision with the understanding that their colleagues will support them on another matter.[2] Such behaviors do not represent consensus.

Plan and Schedule the Work

One feature of the typical team charter is a greater emphasis on ends than on means. Particularly with a project team, the sponsor should specify the desired end and leave the plan for getting there to the team's leader and members. With the desired end or ends in hand, the team can then use time-tested tools to plan the work— and eventually implement the plan. Since many teams are, in fact, project teams, those time-tested tools are the same ones that have been developed and used over the past sixty to seventy years by project managers.

Project management is a process for overseeing a focused, time-bound, goal-oriented effort from start to finish. It involves allocating people and resources, coordinating activities and resource expenditures, and monitoring performance. The typical project has four phases: planning, buildup, implementation, and phaseout. We consider only the first of those, planning, here. It begins with a clarification of objectives.

Clarify Objectives

"Develop a Web site capable of providing fast, accurate, cost-effective product information and fulfillment to our customers." That is how a sponsor might describe the team's objective in the charter. But what exactly does it mean? What is "fast"? How should accuracy be defined? Is one error in 1,000 transactions acceptable, or would one error in 10,000 meet the sponsor's expectations? To what degree must the site be cost effective? These are all questions that must be answered, ideally in consultation with the sponsor. All objectives should be specific and measurable. If they are not, you'll have no way of knowing whether the team has met its objectives. There should also be a time frame within which objectives will be achieved; the project cannot be open-ended.

Note: Appendix A contains a worksheet that can help you define your team project. Like other resources in Appendix A, you can obtain a free downloadable copy of it on the Harvard Business Essentials Web site: www.elearning.hbsp.org/businesstools.

Specify Tasks

Once the objectives are very clear and unanimously accepted, work backward to specify the tasks that need to be completed for all objectives to be met. This is a fill-in-the-blanks exercise in which people address these questions:

- What are all the tasks that must be done for these objectives to be achieved?

- What is the optimal order for accomplishing those tasks? Which can be accomplished independently, and which must be handled in series?

- In what time frame must each task be accomplished?

Table 4-1 illustrates one approach to specifying tasks, their related subtasks, and assignment of time periods. The project in this example case aims to move three Web servers and two databases to a new data center.

As shown in table 4-1, each major task is more fully specified as one or more Level 1 subtasks and is often even further specified as Level 2 subtasks. And each subtask is assigned an estimated time duration, the total of which is twenty-two days. This does not mean that the total time needed to complete the project is twenty-two days, since some tasks can be completed in parallel. For instance, team members could alert the data center about the arrival of new equipment during the same period in which the purchase order is being completed and sent to vendors. Project managers use scheduling tools such as PERT charts (Performance Evaluation and Review Technique) and Gantt charts to slot individual tasks into discrete time blocks, recognizing that some tasks must be handled in a particular series while others tasks are independent. A PERT chart for the data-center project is shown in figure 4-1.

TABLE 4-1

Task Specification

Major Task	Level 1 Subtasks	Level 2 Subtasks	Level 2 Subtask Duration (days)
Obtain Equipment	Purchase 3 servers and 2 databases	Cut purchase order and submit to vendor	5
	Ship equipment to new data center	Alert data center that equipment is slated for arrival	2
Prepare and Implement Equipment	Physically install hardware	Rack and cable equipment and ensure network connectivity	2
	Load operating system		1
	Load applications	Load software, including server software, database applications, and required dependencies	2
	Mirror content to new servers	Copy configurations, transfer files to new servers, and load appropriately	3
Test Equipment	Test machines	Ensure connectivity in the network; check database access and functionality	2
Go Live	Cutover to new data center	Switch Web and database access to new sites	1
	Check data and content integrity	Run predetermined tests to ensure data accuracy	1
Test Again	Let sites burn in for 24 hours and check integrity again		1
Decommission Old Equipment	Remove old equipment from site	Uninstall equipment; erase software and content	1
	Store equipment for future use or sale	Ship equipment back to inventory	1
		Total duration (days)	22

Source: Adapted with permission from Harvard ManageMentor® Project Management (Boston: Harvard Business School Publishing, 2002), 16.

Tips for Creating a Project Schedule

1. Develop a list of specific tasks.

2. Assign a deliverable to each activity—for instance, "prototype for market testing."

3. Use deliverables as a basis for creating a project schedule with realistic milestones and due dates.

4. Identify bottlenecks that could upset the schedule.

5. Determine ways to eliminate bottlenecks, or build in extra time to get around them.

6. Establish control and communications systems for updating and revising the schedule.

7. Keep all stakeholders involved in and informed of the project's progress and any schedule modifications.

Note: Most managers of complex projects use software programs to help with project planning and scheduling. To determine which software is best for your situation, check the latest software reviews and get recommendations from an experienced project manager.

Assign Tasks

In some project-team situations, members join or are assigned to the team prior to the task-specification stage; they organize themselves around the top-level project goals. In other cases, the task specification described is accomplished by a small core of managers and/or functional specialists. Those core individuals consider what must be done and then recruit members capable of handling the various tasks. In either situation, task assignments should be made with these criteria in mind:

• Assign tasks to the individuals best able to do the job.

FIGURE 4-1

PERT Chart

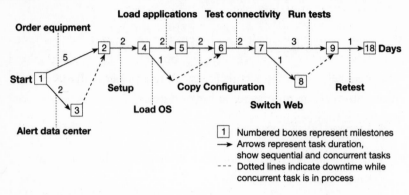

Source: Adapted with permission from Harvard ManageMentor® Project Management (Boston: Harvard Business School Publishing, 2002), 25.

- Make it clear how each assigned task fits with the highest-level team goals—and how those team goals fit with organizational goals.

- As tasks are assigned, also assign the authority and resources needed to complete them.

Define the Measures of Success

Teams should identify a set of specific performance measures that can be used to chart the team's progress toward its goals. The types of measures used depend largely on the specific work; nevertheless, they should reflect the achievement of clear milestones on the road to the team's goals. For example, the project team charged with migrating the company Web servers and databases to a new data center would probably adopt these success measures at a minimum:

- Complete the job in eighteen days or less.

- Provide 99 percent error-free service after switch-over to the new system.

- Stay within initial budget.

In setting team goals, leaders and members should follow this timeless advice: Make the goals challenging but achievable. Or, as Richard Hackman says in his book on teams: "A team's performance hurdle must be not be so high as to be beyond members' reach nor so low as to be uninteresting."[3]

Develop a Budget

Few team efforts are given a blank check. Senior management foresees measurable benefits if the team succeeds, but it also recognizes the associated costs. To keep those costs within an acceptable range, management gives the team limited resources and expects it to accomplish its goals with them. The team creates a budget to make the most of those resources.

A budget is the financial blueprint for the team project. It translates plans into measurable quantities that denote the cost of required resources and the anticipated returns over a period of time—typically the expected life of the project. Most experts agree that unless management is willing to fully fund the anticipated cost of a project, it should not initiate it. Therein lies an important tip for every team leader: If the sponsor has great expectations but will not provide a realistic level of funding or resources, think twice about accepting the job—or fight for what you think is necessary to do the job.

In developing a budget, you must forecast all anticipated costs and revenues (if any). The bulk of project costs falls into the following categories:

- **Personnel.** You will not have to include personnel costs if team members' time is donated by their departments or business units.

- **Outside help.** The fees of consultants, trainers, and other facilitators must be anticipated and figured into the budget.

- **Travel.** Will your team members travel to meeting sites, to customer facilities, or to benchmarking locations? If they will, include the expense in the budget.

- **Training.** Project teams often receive training on team-based
  work, the use of special software, and skill development.

- **Capital expenditures.** Estimate and include the cost of team
  computers, software, communications equipment, and so forth
  if they are not provided by the organization.

- **Research.** Will you have to purchase studies or data to support
  the project? If so, at what cost?

Create Integrating Mechanisms

Simply throwing people into a launch meeting, giving them collective goals, and handing out free T-shirts with a team name and logo
creates a team in name only. Real teams are created through collaborative activities: mainly joint work and idea sharing. You can facilitate these team-building activities through integrative mechanisms:
regularly scheduled meetings, communications links, physical colocation, and social events that build team identification and group
cohesion.

Each of these mechanisms, in effect, encourages people to talk
with one another, share ideas, analyze and critique alternative strategies, and build the bonds of trust and friendship that make team-
based work stimulating and productive.

Generally, physical colocation is one of the most powerful but
least exploited integrative mechanisms. R&D and new-product
teams have found that physical environments can be engineered in
ways that encourage higher creative output. For example, when an
environment is filled with many types of stimuli, and when it provides

physical and electronic links between individuals, it enables people to see new connections and to think more broadly.

In the late 1990s, a team of researchers at MIT's School of Architecture and Planning—the Space and Organization Research Group (SPORG)—began looking at the connection between workspace design and work processes. One of SPORG's more interesting case studies involved a work space that was being developed for a new project team at a Xerox Corporation research center in New York State.[4] There, the space and the work were designed simultaneously and with a high level of coordination. Team members were collocated for easier communication with each other and for closer proximity to the physical equipment that occupied their thoughts and experiments. Lines of movement into, out of, and through the work space were deliberately laid out to create frequent and convenient contact between teammates. Meeting rooms were designed so that physical artifacts in the labs were in sight and accessible. Meetings were open to all.

A small but growing body of research is demonstrating what intuition already tells us—that features of colocation and work-space design, like those designed into the Xerox lab, are linked with work effectiveness. Indeed, modern management's shift toward less formal, team-based ways of working has forced architects and designers to develop spaces that are more adaptable to work-process changes, more concerned with interemployee communication, and more supportive of creative and cognitive patterns of work. This is the logic behind BMW's Munich engineering center, known as FIZ (which stands for *Forschungs und Innovationszentrum*).

FIZ, which opened in 1987, is based on the concept of colocation. It brings together in one site everyone concerned with auto product development, including BMW's suppliers. Approximately 5,000 researchers, engineers, and technicians currently work in FIZ, which is designed around a network that links various groups together. The maximum walking distance between any two FIZ occupants is 150 meters. That encourages physical contact and informal communication between the many people who work toward common objectives.

DaimlerChrysler attempted something very similar—but on twice the scale—when it built its Technology Center in Auburn Hills, Michigan.

What's the nature of your team's workplace? Do its members work out of closed offices where contact with other team members is strictly accidental or requires advance planning? What is the physical distance between the people who should be interacting and sharing ideas on a regular basis? Organizational researchers have known for a long time that the frequency of communication between coworkers decreases dramatically as the physical distance between them increases. As MIT researcher Tom Allen discovered years ago: "People are more likely to communicate with those who are located nearest to them. Individuals and groups can therefore be positioned in ways that will either promote or inhibit communication."[5] Thus, work-space design and the physical location of team members have a major impact on the depth of communication and knowledge sharing.

Authors Marc Meyer and Al Lehnerd underscore the importance of collocation in their book on team-based product-platform development:

> The principles of collocating teams, exposing them to a variety of information, and providing a persistent display of that information, are important. . . . Just bringing team members together into one physical place has been shown to improve communication and information sharing. There, small bits of knowledge and information that by themselves mean nothing can be pieced together with other bits to form meaningful insights. Team collocation also fosters bonding between individual members and the commitment needed for focused, fast, high-risk projects.[5]

One effective approach to the colocation issue—even when moving members' individual work spaces into close proximity is not feasible—is establishment of a *team room*. A team room is a space dedicated to the work of the team and its members. It functions as a space for team meetings, as a place where members can congregate to share ideas, and where all the physical artifacts and records of the team's work can be displayed or kept. The latter may include the following:

- Disassembled competing products

- The team's current prototypes

- Relevant test and research reports

- A specialized library of technical books and journals

The team room may also post these items on the wall:

- A large PERT or Gantt chart that plots the project's current progress and milestones from start to finish

Tips for Making the Most of the Team Room

A team room is the natural setting for team meetings. But you'll only get the full benefits of the space if people make it a regular gathering place. Here are a few things you can do to draw people to the team room on a regular basis:

- Sponsor periodic brown-bag luncheons in the team room. Use a particular topic, a visiting research scientist, a key customer, or an executive from an alliance partner as a magnet to bring people together for these informal sessions.

- Create an informal and comfortable space by eliminating traditional meeting-room furniture in favor of sofas, coffee tables, and lounge chairs.

- Keep plenty of drawing pads and pens on hand to encourage people to sketch out their ideas.

- Include a small refrigerator stocked with soda, juice, and snacks, which will draw team members into the room.

- The original copy of the team charter, signed by the executive sponsor

- The team budget, including current variances

- The names and phone numbers of "friendlies"—nonteam members with important insights who are willing to help the team and its members

This team room should also be equipped with a speakerphone—and perhaps videoconferencing equipment—to accommodate group discussion with off-site members and friendlies. A whiteboard and paper flip chart should complete the setting. Collectively, the team room and its accoutrements facilitate team work and foster team identity.

Establish Norms of Behavior

Turning an assemblage of individuals into an effective team cannot be done overnight. Individuals come to the team effort with personal agendas. Many view their new teammates as competitors for promotions, recognition, and rewards. Still others may harbor personal grudges against one or more of the people with whom they have been thrown together. And there is always an individual or two who lack the social skills required for group work.

Personal agendas, internal competitions, grudges, and poor social skills are present to some degree on every team, and they undermine team effectiveness if they're not contained or neutralized. The diversity of specialties and work styles that you've probably brought to the team through great effort may also make collaboration more difficult. Technical specialists, after all, often speak in an unfamiliar language. One of the best ways of managing these problems is by setting down clear norms of behavior. As described by Katzenbach and Smith, the most critical rules pertain to:

- **Attendance.** Members and leaders must understand that the team cannot make decisions and accomplish its work if individual members fail to show up for meetings or joint work sessions. If you are the leader, people will follow you example. If you are chronically late or absent, they will mimic your behavior.

- **Interruptions.** Decide that cell phones will be off during meetings and work sessions. Taking a call during a team session indicates that the call is more important than what the team is doing.

- **No sacred cows.** Agree that no issues will be protected from discussion. For example, even if it knows that a change will upset a particular executive, a process-reengineering team should not be afraid or reluctant to discuss the issue. Sweeping the executive's possible objections under the table will signal to everyone that the team and its efforts are pointless.

- **Constructive criticism.** Problem solving is bound to produce competing solutions. The champions of these solutions must understand that they are empowered to represent their views but are forbidden to undermine those of others through deception or by withholding relevant data. Team players must also learn how to vent their disagreement with others in constructive ways.

- **Confidentiality.** Some team issues are bound to be sensitive. They will not be discussed freely unless all members have confidence that what is said within the team stays within the team.

- **Action orientation.** Teams are not formed to meet and discuss; those that do are simply gab sessions. Their real purpose is to act and produce results. Make that clear from the very beginning. In the words of Katzenbach and Smith, an action orientation means that "everyone does real work," and "everyone gets assignments and does them."[7]

Later, we'll examine the management issues surrounding norms of behavior at length. But their implementation deserves discussion here because dealing with them explicitly is one of the keys to getting the team off on the right foot.

What should your group's norms of behavior be? That depends on the purpose of the group and the personalities of its members. But certainly any effective set of norms should be clear and concise. They should also include the basics: respect for all members of the group, a commitment to active listening, and an understanding about how to voice concerns and handle conflict.

To guarantee the free flow of ideas, some groups may want to go further—for example, making it explicit that anyone is entitled to disagree with anyone else. They may also want to adopt specific guidelines that

- support calculated risk taking,

- establish procedures about acknowledging and handling failure,

- foster individual expression, and

- encourage a playful attitude.

Whatever norms your group adopts, make sure all the members participate in establishing them—and that everyone is willing to abide by them. Their participation and acceptance will head off many future problems. Also, be aware that norms often emerge in unanticipated ways, even if guidelines are explicitly discussed at the beginning of the team project. For example, if some egos are bruised during the team's initial meeting, you may observe subtle hostility in subsequent interactions between the affected individuals. That hostility will probably manifest itself through second-guessing, criticism, sarcasm, and other counterproductive behaviors. As a leader or team member, you should discourage such behavior by reminding everyone that mutual respect, open discussion, and collaborative behavior is the expected norm.

Summing Up

- Launch your team with an all-team meeting. Everyone should be there, including the sponsor. During that meeting, explain the charter. Stress the importance of the team's goals and how they fit with larger organizational goals.

- Reach agreement on how decisions will be made. Agreement on this will save valuable time during the life of the team and, if people perceive the decision-making process as fair, result in greater acceptance of the decisions actually made.

- In the planning and scheduling phase, begin with clear and specific objectives. Then deconstruct those objectives into manageably sized tasks and subtasks. Estimate a completion time for tasks, and assign them to the individuals best able to do the job.

- As you schedule, identify all the bottlenecks that could throw your plan off track and then think of ways to either accommodate or eliminate them.

- Always know what success will look like. Then craft a set of specific performance measures that can help chart the team's progress.

- Use a budget to control activities. Make sure at the outset that the sponsor has provided a budget adequate to the task. If the budget is too lean, you may have to negotiate with the sponsor for less demanding goals.

- Integrative mechanisms help turn a group of individuals into a real team. Regularly scheduled meetings, communications links, physical collocation, and social events are mechanisms you can use to build team identification, group cohesion, and collaboration.

- If possible, locate team members physically near each other; doing so will create opportunities for interaction and collaboration. Go a step further: Provide a team room where people can mingle, display prototypes, research reports, and share ideas.

- You can smooth over incompatibilities and make the most of personal differences by creating norms of behavior and gaining acceptance of them. Showing up at meetings on time, completing assignments on schedule, helping teammates when help is needed, constructive criticism, and respect for different viewpoints are examples of positive norms of behavior.

Team Management Challenges

Where Leaders Matter

Key Topics Covered in This Chapter

- *Four roles for team leaders*

- *The benefits of team identity, and how to create it*

- *The perils of groupthink*

- *Managing team creativity*

- *Three steps for making the most of conflict*

THIS CHAPTER addresses management and leadership challenges that are unique to teams. Whether you are a team leader or a team member, recognizing these challenges and knowing how to deal with them will make you a better contributor and teammate.

The Leader's Role

One of the most unique management challenges of team-based work is found in the role of the team leader. As explained earlier, the team leader must do many of the traditional manager's chores: assure that the work is properly planned and organized, that it stays on track and on budget, that results and problems are regularly reported to higher authority—in this case, the sponsor—and so forth. The team leader carries a heavier burden of accountability for results than other team members and must report directly to the team sponsor. Leaders should be comfortable and effective in performing these duties and accepting the lion's share of responsibility. But the traditional duty of directing people must be approached differently, for two reasons:

1. Many, if not most, people on the team will have no reporting relationship with the team leader. The leader is not their boss, has no control over their compensation, and may even be junior to some team members. Consider this example: When Lew

Veraldi created Ford Motor Company's Team Taurus in the late 1970s, his inner team circle included the company's car product planning director, chief engineer, and chief designer, none of whom had a reporting relationship with the team leader. Most of these core members outranked the team leader in the corporate pecking order.[1]

2. Directing by the team leader is antithetical to collaborative, team-based work. If the leader intends to tell people what to do, how to do it, and to what standard, the team approach to the job is pointless. The team leader cannot act like the boss and still obtain the benefits of the team.

If the team leader cannot be boss, he or she nevertheless has four important roles to play—each very critical to team success. Those roles are initiator, model, negotiator, and coach. Let's examine each.

Leader As Initiator

The team leader initiates action. Though the effective leader does not tell people what they must do, he or she draws attention to actions that must be taken in order to meet the team's goals. A good team leader is well positioned to initiate action because he or she usually stands somewhat apart from the day-to-day work of the team, a position from which the connections between that work and the higher objectives of the effort can be more readily observed. While members are deeply enmeshed in tasks and problem solving, the leader is in close contact with the expectations of the sponsor, higher management, and external stakeholders. Using evidence and rational argument, the leader encourages members to take the steps needed to meet those larger expectations. This is an important function, particularly when those expectations are in conflict with the personal expectations of individual team members. Consider this example:

Carmen was the leader of an employee team charged with creating a new plan for utilizing floor space in the company's three-story building.

Her boss, the vice president of operations, wanted a plan that made full use of available space while meeting the needs of all departments, each of which had a representative on the team.

In the beginning, each team member had a proprietary interest in carving out as much space as possible or his or her own department, making it a contest in which one department's gain would result in another's loss. So, one by one, each member stated an argument favoring his or her department. Carmen recognized the disastrous potential of this approach and moved quickly to stop it. She proposed that the team shift away from its current territorial debates. "At this early stage," she told her teammates, "we should take a step back from what we've been doing and pursue two different avenues of discussion and inquiry. First, we need to agree on the principles on which our limited space should be allocated. For example, should space be divided on the basis of department head count, activities, budget, or something else? Second, we need to seek alternatives to the way we currently use floor space. Chances are that other organizations have found better ways of using office space. Perhaps we could learn from them through benchmarking."

Team members saw no threat in these suggestions and shifted their energies to the new approach. Eventually, they decided to benchmark several other companies to identify space-saving and space-allocating practices they might adopt.

In this example, Carmen was an action initiator. She didn't tell people what they should do or order them to do it. Instead, she used logical argument to get people moving into useful activities.

Leader As Model

Both traditional managers and team leaders can use their own behavior to shape others' behavior and performance. The big difference is that team leaders must rely more heavily on this tactic, since they cannot use promotions, compensations, and threats of dismissal to influence team members.

Model behavior by the team leader is, in fact, a powerful tool. It sets a standard to which others must rise, if only to avoid seeming ineffective or petty. In Carmen's, for example, her shifting attention from narrow, parochial interests to principles and best practices had a salutary effect on member behavior. The team moved away from self-serving bickering to consider options that would benefit both it and the company.

Leaders can model team behavior in many different ways. If team members need to get out of the office and rub shoulders with customers, an effective leader would not instruct them to do so. Instead, he or she would begin a regular practice of traveling to customer locations, creating customer focus groups, and so forth. Team members would be encouraged to participate. In a word, the leader would model a behavior that had a direct impact on team performance.

Leader As Negotiator

"I'd like Bill to join our process-improvement team," the team leader told Bill's manager. The manager frowned; Bill was one of her best performers. "Being part of the team will involve about four hours of work each week," the team leader continued, "that includes meetings and team assignments."

Managers do not particularly welcome requests like that one. The team has goals, but so do the managers who are asked to contribute skilled employees and other resources; complying with a team leader's request can only make their jobs more difficult. Effective team leaders recognize this and use negotiating skills to get what they need. The executive sponsor can make the job easier by making it clear that the team's goals are important for the company and that the cooperation of managers is expected.

The best way to negotiate with resource providers is to frame the situation in a positive way. Managers being asked to help are likely to see the situation as a zero-sum proposition, so team leaders with negotiating skills will present requests as mutually beneficial. Here's the difference: A zero-sum (or win-lose) negotiation occurs when the parties compete over the distribution of a fixed pool of value, and any gain by one party represents a loss to the other. Most managers, like Bill's, initially see situations in those terms. A mutually beneficial (or integrative) negotiation, on the other hand, occurs when both parties recognize opportunities for gain. If you are a team leader, you will have a better chance of framing your negotiations as mutually beneficial if you do the following:

- Emphasize the higher-level goals of the organization and how successful team action will contribute to them. Doing so underscores a point made earlier in this book—that team goals must be important and aligned with organizational goals.

- Emphasize how the other party will benefit by helping the team—for example, by indicating how the team's success will contribute to the other party's success.

To be a successful negotiator, the team leader must present himself as trustworthy and reliable and the mutual benefits as realistic.

Leader As Coach

A good team leader finds ways to help team members excel. In most cases, this is accomplished through coaching. In his book on team-based work, Richard Hackman states that good coaching helps teams in three ways: first, by enhancing the level of effort that individual members apply to their work; second, by assuring that the work done is appropriate; and third, by helping members make the most of their talents.[2]

Coaching is a two-way activity in which the parties share knowledge and experience in order to maximize a team member's potential and help him or her achieve agreed-upon goals. It is a shared effort in which the person being coached participates actively and willingly. Good team leaders find coaching opportunities in the course of everyday business. Their coaching can help members with many routine activities to make better presentations, to schedule their work, to deal with intrateam conflict, to obtain external resources, to set up a budget, or even to work effectively in a team environment.

Coaching opportunities are especially prevalent within teams because so many of the skills members eventually need are skills they must learn as their projects unfold. For example, an engineer recruited because of her technical capabilities may suddenly find that she must prepare and present a businesslike progress report to the sponsor and senior management. She must develop presentation skills quickly— and coaching by the leader is often the best solution.

If you are a team leader, you and a particular member may agree to form a coaching relationship when both believe that working together will lead to improved performance. Through coaching, you can help the other person do the following:

- Rekindle motivation in the project

- Get back on track if she is having performance problems

- Maximize the person's strengths—for example, build on analytical skills

Managing Versus Coaching

Though managers must often act as coaches, management and coaching are quite different activities, which explains why so many managers find coaching difficult. Here are the principal differences:

Managing focuses on:	Coaching focuses on:
• Telling	• Exploring
• Directing	• Facilitating
• Authority	• Partnerships
• Immediate needs	• Long-term improvement
• Typically seeking a specific outcome	• Being open to many possible outcomes
• Individual subordinates	• Finding and exploiting complementarities with others

- Overcome personal obstacles—for example, reduce a fear of dealing directly with a difficult team member

- Achieve new skills and competencies—for example, learn how to make a better stand-up presentation

- Prepare for new responsibilities—for example, take charge of an ad hoc task force

- Manage herself more effectively—for example, improve time-management skills

Good coaching produces greater job satisfaction and higher motivation. It may also improve your working relationship with the other person, making your job as team leader much easier. Just remember that effective coaching requires mutual agreement. The other person must *want* to do better and must *welcome* your help.

Note: For a how-to approach to effective coaching, see Appendix B.

Informal Leaders

Though researchers give much attention to the role of formal team leaders, much less is said about the informal leaders who do so much to help teams achieve their goals. Informal leaders are the individuals to whom others naturally turn for advice, assurance, and direction in their day-to-day tasks. Every organization has them, even though they are not invested with authority and do not appear as part of the chain of command in organizational charts.

Informal leadership, in some instances, is a consequence of technical expertise. For example, people within a work group look to a particular individual for direction because that individual has the expertise they lack. Or, that person may have exceptional interpersonal skills that the other members lack. For example, while everyone else is content to do his or her job and take on assignments as directed, people in the group look to one individual—an informal leader—to meditate low-level interpersonal conflicts and to guide day-to-day coordination.

Orchestrating Through Collaborative Leadership

Could your company operate without a CEO? Could an army function in the field if all the generals went into retirement? Would your team be effective if it didn't have an identifiable team leader?

New York City's Orpheus Chamber Orchestra, which is based at Carnegie Hall, has no conductor. Yet like other orchestras, it rehearses, performs, and records its music, garnering awards and audience praise along the way. How does it do this? The secret is that the Orpheus is not leaderless. Instead, leadership is distributed through "collaborative leadership." In their study of this unique organization, authors Harvey Seifter and Peter Economy have distilled eight principles for collaborative leadership:

- Give power to the people who do the work.

- Make individuals responsible for output and quality.

- Give everyone clear roles.

- Share and rotate leadership.

- Make teamwork horizontal.

- Learn to listen, and learn to talk.

- Seek consensus.

- Display passionate commitment to the mission.

Would collaborative leadership work in your organization—or in your team? To find out, read the book.

SOURCE: Harvey Seifter and Peter Economy, *Leadership Ensemble* (New York: Times Books, 2001).

If you are the formal leader of your team, you will be more successful and your job will be easier if you do the following:

- Identify the informal leaders within your team. You can identify them through both their behavior and the deference they receive from others.

- Ensure that informal leaders understand team goals, know why they are important, and accept those goals as their own. You can do this by cultivating good relationships with these people, and by using those relationships to communicate the big picture to others.

- Give informal leaders ample opportunities to contribute. For example, use informal leaders to head up ad hoc task forces, to arrange off-site meetings, and so forth.

If you are the team leader, don't be surprised if the team's informal leaders have more influence than you among the other members. Don't fret about this, and don't resent it. Instead, use their influence to your advantage.

Encouraging Team Identity

In his role as initiator, the team leader must tackle the job of creating a team identity—the psychic glue that holds people together. Without that identity, you won't have a team.

Remember the last time you rode in a crowded elevator. Chances are that four or five people surrounded you, most total strangers. Two were probably sharing a private conversation; the rest were probably staring at the floor indicator or at their shoes—anything that would help them avoid eye contact with their fellow passengers. Though all were headed in the same direction and shared the same confined space, you certainly were not a team. There was no bond or sense of shared purpose between the people on that elevator.

In some respects, newly formed teams suffer from the same lack of identity. By one means or another individual members are selected to work on a project, but until they have opportunities to interact, to discuss a common goal, or to join forces in attacking a problem, they are not much different than the gaggle of elevator strangers just described.

The Benefits of Team Identity

One of the truly important challenges of team management is the task of transforming a group of disconnected individuals into a team with a common identity and a common purpose. Why is team identity important? Two reasons. First, a team identity encourages its members to see themselves as mutually accountable for results—perhaps the single most important contributor to team performance. That sense of mutual accountability eliminates the "I did my share" attitude that weakens performance. When people feel mutually accountable for results, they pitch in to help teammates who are struggling or falling behind. Poor performers feel peer pressure to do better. These are the kinds of behavior that have made employees at Nucor Corporation incredibly productive steel-workers. When a problem occurs within one of Nucor's many work teams, people don't say, "That's not my problem" and then sit around until the problem is fixed. Instead, they join hands to get production rolling. Their paychecks depend on it. It is the very same behavior that urges Southwest Airlines flight crews and gate personnel to pitch in to get their planes loaded and in the air with the least delay. In both cases, people feel mutually accountable for results. They are not inclined to say, "That's not my job" when a problem occurs or when a task must be done.

Team identity and mutual accountability go hand in hand. "No group ever becomes a team until it can hold itself accountable as a team," according to Jon Katzenbach and Douglas Smith. As they explain: "At its core, team accountability is about the sincere promises we make to ourselves and others, promises that underpin two critical aspects of effective teams: commitment and trust."[3]

The second important reason for engendering team identity is that it evokes a higher level of commitment and effort from members.

The military refers to this as small-group cohesion. It knows that soldiers whose identities are deeply connected with their units will hold together and perform better as they confront the stresses of combat. Individual soldiers know that they are not alone, that they're members of a "band of brothers" with a common interest in survival and victory. In this spirit, they will often take heroic steps to support each other, in some cases to the point of sacrificing their own lives.

In the business context, team identity manifests itself in a greater willingness to collaborate, share information, make a greater effort, make joint decisions, and put team goals ahead of personal goals. Create this sense of identity within your team, and the burden of team leadership will be a lot lighter.

Fostering Team Identity

Obviously, team identity is important. But how can it be created or enhanced? You probably know part of the answer from your own experience. If you were a Boy Scout or Girl Scout, you wore a uniform that identified you as a member of the group, and you recited an oath affirming your dedication to a set of values embraced by your fellow Scouts. If you became a punk rocker, you gladly set aside your Nikes and jeans for black leather, spiked hair, and a nose ring. In both cases, outward symbols identified you with a group and the things it represented. Work teams attempt the same with team T-shirts and hats. Such emblems are useful, but minimally so. Identification through common goals and values is much more powerful.

The team-identity issue contains a vexing paradox: The diversity that gives many teams real effectiveness can frustrate team identity. As Jeffrey Polzer writes: "[D]ifferences among team members are the sources of varied ideas, perspectives, and skills that can improve the team's ability to make good decisions and accomplish its work. When the components of the team's task are interdependent, team members need to integrate their differentiated work efforts." Unfortunately, diversity may act as a wedge, hindering social interactions that help team members to integrate their work. Poltzer continues, "Indeed, the very differences that give teams the potential for high

performance can make it difficult for group members to work together because they may be the source of misunderstandings, differ-
ing assumptions, stereotypes, biases, and related disruptions."[4]

The potential problems associated with diversity are many. At the
level of culture, for example, American members of a cross-national
R&D team may find the formality of their German counterparts an-
noying. Likewise, the Germans may not appreciate the informality
and lack of deference exhibited by their North American colleagues.
A German with an advanced degree, for example, usually expects to
be addressed as "Doctor," not as "Hey, Hans." Both contingents of the
team are likely to tell mocking jokes behind their counterparts'
backs—jokes they would never tell to the other's faces. Racial diversity can likewise add an element of edginess, if not distrust and discomfort, to a team.

The challenge for team leaders is to enhance team identity without suppressing the valuable differences among team members that
make them diverse. So what can you do to overcome the adverse
consequences of diversity and foster team identity? The most important thing is to emphasize activities and goals that touch individual
values, experiences, and personal interests. For example:

- Be selective in recruiting. Bring in people who see the team's
  goals as important and worthwhile. These people will be more
  predisposed to concentrating on achieving goals than to thinking about differences within the team.

- Engage members in activities they find interesting and valuable.
  This too will keep them focused on the thing that matters: results.

- Find opportunities to recognize the skills and contributions of
  individual members. Doing so will make those individuals feel
  appreciated, valued, and part of the group.

- Publicly recognize the value of differences and how they serve
  the common goal.

- Create opportunities for members to know each other.
  Whether it's through off-site recreation, lunches in the team

room, or something else, give people opportunities to know each other at a personal level. Doing so will enable them to cut through stereotypes (like, "those engineers are hard to work with") and find bases for collaborative work.

- Get people working together! Nothing builds team identity like working together side by side.

Be particularly attentive to new members. They are bound to feel like outsiders at first. If you've ever joined a club or athletic team whose members all knew each other and enjoyed many common experiences, you know the feeling. You were the outsider—the odd-ball. The regulars all seemed comfortable with each other; you, the newcomer, felt isolated—not one of the group.

On a team, new members generally don't contribute fully until they have gotten to know their coworkers and have learned how to interact and apply their talents. The leader and members can shorten this unproductive period by making the newcomer feel welcome and by getting him or her quickly engaged in team projects. Don't expect this new person to figure out which end is up. If it seems appropriate, plan a little social event around his or her arrival.

In the end, anything you do to foster team identity will pay dividends in team performance.

Guarding Against Groupthink

Every close-knit team can fall victim to a pattern of thought called *groupthink*. And the more close-knit the team is, the higher the risk. Irving Janus, the late Yale psychologist who coined the term, defined groupthink as a way of thinking that people may adopt when they are members of a cohesive or homogeneous group; in particular, a group whose members seek unanimity of thought to the point that they cannot consider alternative ideas. Groupthink differs from the false consensus described earlier in this book. In a situation of false consensus, everyone nods in agreement without truly agreeing. People do this (a) when they are tired of opposing issues and want to move on to something else or (b) when they implicitly indicate "I'll go along with you on this matter if you'll support me on another issue." In contrast, groupthink is based on true consensus.

Groupthink is the convergence of thinking around a norm that everyone in the group believes to be correct. Unfortunately, that convergence is driven less by objectivity than by social psychological pressures. When all members identify strongly with the team, they may highlight similarities (while suppressing differences) and strive to agree with each other. Doing so can engender cooperation, a good thing, but can inadvertently curtail critical thinking and debate. The impulse for team agreement and unity takes priority over objectivity.

Social psychologists have long observed how opinion within groups tends to converge as group members become aware of their peers' opinions. For example, when polled separately about their forecasts of future interest rates, the collective opinion of economists generally produces a broad range of rates. Once they learn what their peers are forecasting, however, the range miraculously tends to narrow, with most forecasts clustering close to the mean. Such convergence is explained by the reluctance of individuals—perhaps due to a lack of self-confidence—to make forecasts that are out of step with others. Perhaps you've observed the same phenomenon in group meetings you've attended.

Convergence of opinion is important for teams, especially with respect to goals, how decisions should be made, and the norms of group behavior. It's hard to function effectively without agreement on those issues. But convergence that escalates to groupthink is dangerous. Diversity of views gives way to homogeneity, which creates an illusion of certitude. Those who "think otherwise" may even be reeducated or pushed out. Here are some symptoms of groupthink:

- An illusion of invulnerability prevails.

- Leaders are insulated or protected from contradictory evidence.

- Members accept confirming data and reject data that fails to fit with their views.

- Alternatives are not considered.

- Individuals whose views are out of step with the majority are discounted or demonized.

Do you recognize any of those symptoms in your team? If you do, leaders and members must take steps to welcome a diversity of thoughtful ideas. One way to do this is to empower a team of bright and respected people to objectively represent dissenting ideas and data. The team should examine and report back on every one of its key assumptions. Another anti-groupthink measure is to appoint a respected and qualified person to the role of devil's advocate. This person will challenge the assumptions and conclusions of the majority. He or she will also represent dissenting views and force other members to deal with facts and ideas that conflict with their own.

Managing Team Creativity

Creativity is an important element in most team-based work. Self-managed teams must think of ways to do the same job faster, better, and cheaper. And project teams are brought together to handle unique problems and opportunities—things that fall outside the realm of routine practice. Both types of teams benefit from the creativity of their members.[5]

Most people think of creativity as a very individual phenomenon. Creativity is often an individual act, but many innovations are products of creative groups. The transistor developed by scientists at Bell Labs is just one example. Many of the breakthroughs achieved by Thomas Edison and George Eastman were likewise products of those two recognized inventors *and* the various technicians and engineers who worked with them. Groups can often achieve greater creative output than individuals working alone because they bring a greater sum of varied competencies, insights, experiences, and energy to the effort. But in order to reap greater output, groups must have the right composition of thinking styles and technical skills, which, in most cases, means a diversity of styles and skills. That variety has several benefits:

- Individual differences can produce the creative friction that sparks new ideas.

- Diversity of thought and perspective are a safeguard against groupthink—that is, the tendency of individual thought to converge for social reasons around a particular point of view.

- Diversity of thought and skills gives good ideas more opportunities to develop.

Team leaders thus need to consider how teams are staffed and how the individuals within them communicate.

Paradoxical Characteristics

The creative team exhibits paradoxical characteristics. It shows tendencies of thought and action that we'd assume to be mutually exclusive or contradictory. For example, to do its best work, a team needs deep knowledge of subjects relevant to the problem it's trying to solve, and a mastery of the processes involved. But at the same time, the team needs fresh perspectives that are unencumbered by the prevailing wisdom or established ways of doing things. Often called a "beginner's mind," this is the newcomers' perspective: people who are curious, even playful, and willing to ask anything—no matter how naïve the question may seem—because they don't know what they don't know. Thus, bringing together contradictory characteristics can catalyze new ideas.

Table 5-1 describes a number of seemingly contradictory characteristics that a group must have to maximize its creative potential. Many people mistakenly assume that creativity is a function only of the elements in the left column of the table: the beginner's mind, freedom, play, and improvisation. But a blend of the left *and* the right columns is needed. This paradoxical combination is confusing and disturbing to managers who feel uncomfortable in an environment that lacks a high level of order and linear activity. Accepting this environment is the first step toward success in managing creativity.

TABLE 5-1

The Paradoxical Characteristics of Creative Groups

Beginner's Mind	A team needs fresh, inexperienced perspectives as well as skilled expertise. Bringing in outsiders is often a useful way to provide the necessary balance of perspective.	**Experience**
Freedom	A team must work within the confines of real business needs—and in alignment with the company's strategy. But it also needs latitude—some degree of freedom to determine *how* it will achieve the strategy and address the business needs.	**Discipline**
Play	Creativity thrives on playfulness, but business must be conducted professionally. Provide time and space for play, but clarify the appropriate times and places.	**Professionalism**
Improvisation	Plan your project carefully, but remember that projects do not always go as planned. Encourage team members to look for ways to turn unexpected events into opportunities. Keep plans flexible enough to incorporate new or improved ideas.	**Planning**

Source: Harvard Business Essentials: Managing Creativity and Innovation (Boston: Harvard Business School Press, 2003), 85.

Managing Divergent and Convergent Thinking

Anytime you circle a team around a task and encourage its members to debate and plan how that task should be handled, two types of thinking emerge: divergent and convergent. Neither is particularly important in a traditional work group, where the manager does the thinking and planning and the employees do the work. But both are important in team environments. If you are the team leader, you must be able to recognize and harmonize these two complementary types of thinking.

As described by Dorothy Leonard and Walter Swap in their book on group creativity, *divergent thinking* represents a departure from familiar or established ways of seeing and doing, allowing people to see old things in new ways.[6] The virtues of divergent thinking seem intuitively obvious. If we continually observe an object from the same vantage point and in the same lighting conditions, we are bound to have a fixed—and limited—impression of that object. Change the lighting or the viewing angle, however, and perceptions will change. They will become more complete—more nuanced. Seeing things from an unfamiliar perspective makes it possible to develop insights and new ideas. But are those insights valuable? That's what *convergent thinking* attempts to answer. Convergent thinking helps channel the results of divergent thinking into concrete proposals for action. As ideas generated by divergent thinking are communicated to others, they are evaluated to determine which are genuinely novel and worth pursuing. That's convergent thinking, and it's one of the benefits of team-based work. Without convergent thinking, the creative person working alone could easily pursue an idea that would only eat up time and resources and lead to a dead end.

In moving from divergent to convergent thinking, a team stops emphasizing what is novel and starts emphasizing what is useful. Convergence sets limits, narrowing the field of solutions within a given set of constraints. How do you determine those constraints? The culture, mission, priorities, and high-level concept of your company and project all contribute to the answer. They help you rule out options that lie beyond the scope of your project.

Here are some questions that a new product team, for example, might ask as it applies convergent thinking to a range of possible courses of action:

- Which functions are essential (from the customer's point of view) and which are only nice to have?

- What criteria are determined by the company's values? For example, Fisher-Price groups insist that its new toys be mom-friendly—since most toys are purchased by mothers.

- What are the cost constraints?

- What are the size or shape constraints?

- How soon must the project be completed?

- In what ways must the product or service be compatible with existing products or services?

Tips for Improving Convergent Thinking

Work groups are often tempted to converge quickly on what appears to be the single best solution and to mute any dissent. It's the team leader or manager's job to prevent both. Consider these suggestions:

- Insist on an incubation period during which people can experiment with the various options. Some options will not seem so promising after people have thought about them for a week or two.

- Appoint an official devil's advocate to challenge all assumptions associated with the group's favored options.

- Assure that dissent is tolerated and protected, and that dissenters have the freedom to voice contrary views. Otherwise, groupthink may take control of future decisions.

Managing Conflict

Like any other set of individuals, teams present opportunities for conflict. In fact, the diversity of thinking and skills assembled within teams raises the potential for conflict. Different thinking styles and professional disciplines do not necessarily produce harmony. For example, engineers on a product-development team may be impatient with a finance specialist who is concerned with the cost of their proposals. "This guy doesn't know a screwdriver from a drill press," they complain to one another. "He's slowing us down." In other cases, one group of team members may have a process-reengineering plan that others strongly oppose. "That's crazy," they complain to the team leader. "If we did that we'd be making a bad process worse—and wasting our time." This type of conflict is commonplace and expected. Since it cannot be—and shouldn't be—eliminated, the team must learn to manage and make the most of conflict.

To turn conflict from a negative to a positive force, team members must listen to each other, be willing to understand different viewpoints, and objectively question each other's assumptions. At the same time, team leaders must prevent that conflict from becoming personal or from going underground, where resentment can simmer. Here are three steps for making the most of conflict:

1. **Create a climate that makes people willing to discuss difficult issues.**

   Disagreement builds and produces no positive result when people fail to deal with the issue at the conflict's source. Some people call this matter "the moose on the table." It's there, but nobody wants to acknowledge it or to talk about it. Make it clear that you *want* the tough issues aired, and that *anyone* can point out a moose.

2. **Facilitate the discussion.**

   How do you deal with a moose once it has been identified? Use the following guidelines:

   - First, stop whatever you are doing and acknowledge the issue, even if only one person sees it.

   - Refer back to group norms on how people treat each other.

   - Encourage the person who identified the moose to be specific.

   - Keep the discussion impersonal. The point is not to assign blame—discuss *what* is impeding progress, not *who*.

   - If the issue involves someone's behavior, encourage the person who identified the problem to explain how the behavior affects him or her, rather than to make assumptions about the motivation behind the behavior. For example, if someone is not completing work when promised, you might say, "When your work is not completed on time, the rest of us are unable to meet our deadlines," not "I know you are not really excited about this product."

   - If someone is not providing necessary leadership, you might say, "When you don't provide us with direction, we spend a lot of time trying to guess what you want. If we guess wrong, we waste time," not "You don't seem to have any idea what we should be doing on this project."

3. **Move toward closure by discussing what can be done.**

- Leave with some concrete suggestions for improvement, if not a solution, to the problem.

- If the subject is too sensitive and discussions are going nowhere, consider adjourning your meeting until a specified later date so that people can cool down. Or bring in a facilitator.

A Conflict-Reducing Exercise

In many cases, the cause of conflict between individuals or groups is a failure to listen. While one side is explaining its point of view and laying out its supporting data, the other side is simply waiting for a chance to jump in and present its view. Each side, in effect, talks past the other. The chance of reducing conflict is almost always improved when this behavior stops and when each side listens closely and makes a real effort to understand the other's position.

Here's a role-playing exercise that your team can use to promote the understanding that reduces conflict. If Jane is the spokesperson for one point of view and Fred is her most vocal critic, have them reverse roles. Require Fred to articulate Jane's position, and ask Jane to represent the opposition. To play their new roles effectively, of course, they must learn the details—the very details they have ignored so far. Ask each of them to meet with the other and try to internalize the other's best arguments and supporting data. This exercise may not change anybody's mind, but if the participants are fair-minded they will come away with greater respect for the other side's position. That respect will take the hard edge off the conflict and facilitate resolution that both sides can support.

Summing Up

- Being a team leader is not the same as being a manager. The team leader usually cannot be the boss. Instead, he or she must produce results by acting as initiator, model, negotiator, and coach.

- Team identity holds people together and supports greater mutual effort. Team identity and mutual accountability go hand in hand.

- To foster team identity, be very selective in recruiting members. Bring in people who see the team's goals as important and worthwhile. Then engage those members in activities they find interesting and valuable. Recognize the skills and contributions of individual members. Create opportunities for members to get to know each other at a personal level.

- Avoid groupthink. Two approaches for doing so are (1) to empower a team of respected people to objectively represent dissenting ideas and (2) to appoint a devil's advocate to challenge the assumptions and conclusions of the majority.

- Many innovations are products of creative groups' greater manpower and varied competencies, insights, and experiences.

- One way to tap the creative potential of a team is to bring together diverse thinking styles and skills.

- To make the most of creativity, a team leader must harmonize divergent and convergent thinking.

- Divergent thinking represents a breaking away from familiar or established ways, allowing people to see and do old things in new ways. Convergent thinking helps channel the results of divergent thinking into concrete proposals for action.

6

Operating As a Team

Putting Ideas to Work

Key Topics Covered in This Chapter

- *How to check for collaboration and information sharing*

- *How to defuse conflict between an individual and the team*

- *Using achievable milestones to pace the work and motivate people*

- *The importance of team learning and how to enhance it*

- *Performance evaluation—of the team and its members*

ONCE A TEAM is launched and its members get down to business, it needs to start acting like a team—and acting effectively. Members will naturally develop patterns of collaboration and interaction, but unfortunately, they may not be what you expect or want. Depending on the people involved, team patterns may be very productive, or they might be unproductive and divisive. It's up to the leader and members to monitor these patterns and intervene when necessary to assure that people are working together productively and that the methods of collaboration and interaction will carry them toward their goals and keep them on schedule.

This chapter examines key aspects of team operations and how you can make them work better.

Keeping an Eye on Team Processes

As some point, either before or shortly after launch, all the team's required tasks will have been identified, assigned to appropriate members, and scheduled for completion. This upfront job of planning, assigning, and scheduling requires good powers of goal analysis. It appeals to people with organizing skills and problem-solving minds. Representing all the tasks within a PERT or Gantt chart makes it all appear logical—even easy. Unfortunately, something is missing from these charts: *team processes*. And these processes are generally the most important factors in team-based work. They are the glue that holds everything together.

Team processes can be defined as collaboration and information sharing among members and leaders. They may be either effective or dysfunctional. Effective collaboration and information sharing put the team on the road to goal achievement. If they are dysfunctional, even excellent performances by individuals are unlikely to produce the team performance expected by the sponsor and organization. If you're the team leader, it's your job to pay close attention to team processes. You must determine whether they are working well or poorly. If they are working poorly, you must find the cause of the problem and address it with appropriate interventions.

Collaborative Behavior

Have you ever watched a basketball game in which one player took a shot just about every time he got his hands on the ball? His teammates passed the ball whenever they were badly positioned or closely guarded by opposing players. But the "ball hog" never passed, even when a teammate was open and within easy striking distance of the basket. This illustrates one type of noncollaborative behavior you have to watch for on your team. Specifically, check to see whether team members are sharing the work as they move toward their goals, or if one individual is trying to do it all. Even if a prima donna is a high performer, his or her behavior will discourage participation by others and slow overall progress. Also, watch for anyone, including a team leader, who

- appears to be taking undue credit for the team's accomplishments,

- is always pressing to get a larger share of team resources, or

- is secretive or unwilling to share information.

Such behaviors will undermine the commitment of others and reduce team cohesion, and everyone on the team has a responsibility to change them. You'll recognize healthy collaboration when you observe team members doing the following:

- Putting team interests above their own

- Giving part of their budgets, lab time, or other resources to teammates who can use it more effectively

How to Have Healthy Conflict

Smart managers know that conflict over issues is natural and even necessary. Teams in which individuals challenge each other's thinking ultimately develop a more complete understanding of their choices, create a richer range of options, and make better decisions. The challenge is to keep conflict constructive—to keep it from degenerating to the level of interpersonal attacks.

Based on their research on the interplay of conflict, politics, and decision-making speed within teams, Kathleen Eisenhardt, Jean Kahwajy, and L. J. Bourgeois III have distilled six tactics used by high-performing management teams:

1. They work with more, rather than less, information.

2. They develop multiple alternatives to enrich debate.

3. They rally around goals.

4. They make an effort to inject humor into the workplace.

5. They maintain a balanced corporate power structure.

6. They resolve issues without forcing a consensus.

Tactics 1 and 2 get people to focus on issues instead of personalities. Tactics 3 and 4 frame decisions as collaborations aimed at achieving the best possible solution for the organization. Finally, tactics 5 and 6 establish a sense of fairness and equity in the process. If conflicts lack that sense of fairness, people will not accept decisions as legitimate.

SOURCE: Adapted with permission from Kathleen M. Eisenhardt, Jean L. Kahwajy, and L. J. Bourgeois III, "How Management Teams Can Have a Good Fight," *Harvard Business Review,* July–August 1997, 77–85.

- Showing an eagerness to share credit for successes

- Putting in extra hours on team projects

- Settling differences and working out schedules among themselves

- Preventing disagreements from becoming personal

The last point deserves special attention because personal animosity is a major team wrecker. According to expert Jeffrey Polzer, relationship conflict distracts people from their work and causes them to reduce their commitment to the team and its goals. "Some teams can't get through a meeting without an angry outburst, overt criticism, and hard feelings," he writes. "When this happens, team members may respond by withdrawing from debates, attempting instead to preserve their relationships by avoiding confrontation."[1]

If you observe this kind of relationship conflict, take action to stop it. Do whatever is necessary to bring the feuding parties together, examine the conflict in an objective manner, and seek a resolution. If either or both parties are too stubborn or too single-minded to work things out, think about getting those individuals off the team.

Defusing Conflict Between an Individual and the Team

In some cases, one team member's behavior causes difficulty for the team or one of its working members. That behavior can take many forms. Consider these hypothetical examples:[2]

- Jason has a personal dislike for Ernestine because of some event that happened before they became members of the team. He manifests his dislike by disagreeing with any proposal Ernestine makes at meetings. Jason's relentless opposition has caused Ernestine to become more passive at meetings, where she now speaks up only rarely.

- John has been a manager with the company for many more years than has Harold, the formal team leader. He is also higher up in the pecking order than Harold, though the two work in

different departments. Whether by intention or a habit of taking charge, John acts as though he's the boss. Aggressive in his
behavior, he wrests control of team meetings by insisting on
agenda changes and dominating the conversation. John has
even taken to sitting at the head of the meeting table. At other
times, he calls individual team members with instructions on
how he'd like them to handle their tasks.

- Cynthia was eager to join the office relocation team because of
  her strong interest in obtaining more efficient space for her
  sales support unit, which was currently crammed into a rabbit
  warren of disconnected workrooms. The company's plan to
  move to a new office building created the possibility of cor-
  recting that situation. Unfortunately, Cynthia has not been acting as a team player. Instead, she has used her membership to
  lobby for her department's interest. She recently ran afoul of
  the other team members by running to the company's chief
  operating officer to complain about how the team was not giving her what she needed.

Each of these individuals is in conflict with his or her team, and that
conflict undoubtedly has a negative impact on the work. Each must
be dealt with—and the sooner the better.

There are two different approaches for handling conflict-causing
individuals: through open team discussion and through private channels. In the team-discussion approach, every member may comment
about every other team member regarding behavior they like, behavior that causes problems for them, how each person could behave
differently, and what the team needs from each person to be successful. Team members then commit to changing their behavior as a
result of that feedback. This approach takes time, substantial group
trust, and facilitative skills to work most effectively.

In the private approach, a facilitator or team member whose role
is to help maintain team relationships meets privately with the individual who exhibits problem behavior. In this meeting, the facilitator

- describes the specific problematic behavior,

- states the impact of the behavior,

- offers a specific alternative behavior, and

- describes the consequences if the problem behavior continues.

With either approach, it is helpful to set up a time to review progress and support the individual's attempts to change behavior.

Information Sharing

One of the great and commonplace failures of organizational life is the failure to share information. Someone knows something that could help a coworker but does not think to share it. A department has information in its database that, if combined with data held by another department, would produce a revelation. Yet out of carelessness, separate information systems, or simply a wish to control information, data is not shared. Instead, it's kept in separate pockets in the organization and does not always get around to the people who could use it. In other cases, information is deliberately withheld from the team by departments that are hostile to its goals or that view the data as proprietary and a source of organizational power.

As you observe team processes, be alert to both the quality and quantity of the information being shared. Ask yourself these questions:

- Are team members volunteering all relevant information to each other?

- Is anything being withheld?

- Is the information received valid and timely?

- What about other units in the organization—are they providing the information the team needs to do its job?

Answering no to any of these questions should prompt action by the team and its leadership.

One chronic problem with organizational information sharing—and one that affects team projects—is the *data silo*. This refers to the practice of maintaining separate databases within different organizational functions. For example, the marketing and sales department may have a customer database that cannot be accessed from the manufacturing or logistics functions. Project teams would likewise be unable to access the information held in this database. Silo databases are often a legacy of an earlier era of information technology. If they exist in your company, the team must find ways of accessing the information it needs, perhaps by recruiting members from departments that hold essential information. Reforming the IT system of the company is not something you can or should tackle unless it is within the scope of the team charter.

Winning One Bite at a Time

Have you ever heard the question, How do you eat an elephant? It is often used to provoke thinking about planning large tasks. The prospect of eating an elephant is overwhelming at first. It seems impossible. The clever answer to that question is, First, cut it into bite-sized pieces. Analogously, dividing a huge task into small, manageable pieces gives people hope that they can handle it, given sufficient time and resources.

We've already explored the business of deconstructing team goals into their underlying tasks, and scheduling and assigning those tasks. That process is how big, difficult jobs are made manageable, and it is part of work planning that should take place in the earliest phase of team-based work. We haven't discussed, however, how a team can use these bits and pieces of work to stay motivated in the operating phase.

If you are a team leader, use the completion of various tasks scheduled in the PERT or Gantt chart as milestones. These bite-sized pieces of your project will, in most cases, take less than a month to complete. (See table 6-1 for a prototype Gantt chart.) To keep people motivated, get them to stop worrying about the enormity of the project and to start focusing on the most immediate milestones. Then find ways to celebrate those milestones as they are achieved; doing so will help people feel good about what they've been able to accomplish and will energize them to attack the next bite-sized task. Here are just a few suggestions for these celebrations:

TABLE 6-1

Project Gantt Chart

Tasks or Activities	4/8–4/14	4/15–4/21	4/22–4/28	4/29–5/5	5/6–5/12	5/13–5/19	5/20–5/26
Install new servers							
Obtain equipment	▓						
Implement equipment		▓					
Test equipment		▓	▓				
Go live with new equipment				▓	▓	▓	
Repeat testing				▓	▓		
Decommission old equipment						▓	
Evaluate process							▓

Source: Harvard ManageMentor® Project Management (Boston: Harvard Business School Publishing, 2002), 26.

- A catered lunch in the team "war room"—paid for by the team sponsor, of course

- A picnic and ball game at a local park

- A party at the team leader's house

The bigger the achievement, the bigger the celebration—and vice versa.

Note: The appendixes at the end of this book contain two items that can help you as you operate your team: "Project Progress Report" and "Team Troubleshooting Guide." You can obtain free downloadable copies of the Project Progress Report form from the Harvard Business Essentials Web site, which is located at www.elearning. hbsp.org/businesstools.

Keeping Team Results on Schedule

Are you having trouble keeping your team's progress on track? Is it falling behind schedule? If it is, here are some things you can do:

- **Demand compliance.** If people have committed to results according to a particular schedule, remind them of their pledge and hold them to it.

- **Offer incentives.** If you have the resources, offer bonuses or other incentives for on-time completion of the work.

- **Enlist more resources.** If feasible, deploy more equipment or people to the lagging tasks.

Sometimes it may not be possible to keep tasks from falling behind schedule. In these cases, consider these approaches:

- **Renegotiate.** Talk to the concerned parties (the team sponsor and lagging team members) about increasing the budget or extending the timeline of the project or a particular part of it.

- **Narrow the scope of the team's objectives.** If the timing of team deliverables cannot be extended, negotiate with the sponsor on noncritical aspects of the objectives that would be eliminated.

SOURCE: Harvard ManageMentor® on Project Management (Boston: Harvard Business School Publishing, 2002), 40.

Supporting Team Learning

The benefits of team-based work generally take time to develop. Why? Because people have to learn how to work together—and that takes time, especially when people are brought together from different departments. If you've played on a sports team, you probably know how clumsy and ineffective people seem during their first practice sessions and early competitions. Each player approaches the game with a different rhythm. No one knows yet how teammates will handle situations. There are many mistakes and lots of fumbling around. Most of those problems go away as people practice together and face competitors on the field. Teammates learn how to work together.

A group of academic researchers confirmed the team-learning effect in a study of National Basketball Association players. As they wrote: "[T]acit group-level knowledge is manifest in players' learning the nuances of playing together. This is context-dependent knowledge that each member of the team develops about the details of how other members of the team play basketball. Learning derives from the experience of playing together." According to these researchers, the knowledge gained through team play allows individual players to anticipate the actions their teammates will take in the split-second decision making that characterizes a fast break or defensive switch.[3]

Workplace teams likewise use learning to develop the interpersonal coordination and the new skills that make them more effective. Per Richard Hackman: "Over time, members come to know one another's special strengths and weaknesses and become highly skilled in coordinating their activities, anticipating one another's next moves and initiating appropriate responses to them even as those moves are occurring."[4] The wise team leader understands the importance of learning and creates conditions that foster adaptation and rapid learning. But how can that be done?

Experience tells us that some teams learn faster than others. Why is this? Can team leaders do something to accelerate the rate of learning? A 2001 study by Amy Edmondon, Richard Bohmer, and Gary Pisano attempted to answer that last question. They observed sixteen cardiac surgery teams to determine why some teams learned new surgical procedures faster than others. The teams had identical complements of surgeons, nurses, and anesthesiologists and had the very same aim: to implement a new, minimally invasive form of open-heart surgery. Nevertheless, some teams were much faster in learning the new procedures. Some teams extracted disproportionate amounts of learning from each surgical experience. But why? The investigators found that success in learning was influenced by three factors:

1. How teams were put together (team design). Lesson: When you select people for the team, put a premium on people who are eager to learn—and who learn quickly.

2. How they drew on their experiences. Lesson: Periodically ask the team, "What can we learn from what we just did?"

3. The extent to which team leaders who actively managed their teams' learning effort.[5] Lesson: Set up opportunities for people to experiment.

Becoming a Learning Leader

Creating an environment conducive to team learning isn't hard; but it does require a team leader to act quickly. Social psychologists have shown that people watch their supervisors carefully for cues on how team members are expected to behave. These impressions form early in the life of a group or project. To set the right tone, team leaders must:

- **Be accessible.** In order to make clear that others' opinions are welcomed and valued, the leader must be available, not aloof.

- **Ask for input.** An atmosphere of information sharing can be reinforced by an explicit request from the team leader for contributions from members.

- **Serve as a "fallibility model."** Team leaders can further foster a learning environment by admitting their mistakes to the team. One surgeon in [a study on cardiac surgery teams] explicitly acknowledged his shortcomings. "He'll say, 'I screwed up. My judgment was bad in that case,'" a team member reported. That signaled to others on the team that errors and concerns could be discussed without fear or punishment.

SOURCE: Amy Edmondon, Richard Bohmer, and Gary Pisano, "Speeding Up Team Learning," *Harvard Business Review*, October 2001, 10.

Not surprisingly, factor 3—the leadership role—greatly influenced the other two. Fast-learning teams had surgeon-leaders who took an active part in selecting team members, looking not simply for technical qualifications but for an ability to work well with others and a willingness to speak up to higher-status teammates. These same leaders insisted on keeping their teams intact. Slower-learning teams treated members as interchangeable; they figured that medical qualifications mattered but the experience of working together did not.

The bottom line of this study is that a premium should be placed on people who can and will learn from every experience.

Evaluating Performance

Performance evaluation is a necessary part of team operations. As in any other type of work that takes place over weeks, months, or years, team-based work must be periodically evaluated—to identify what is going well and what work is falling behind schedule or veering off course. These evaluations can be used to reward success and to identify points where intervention by the team leader and members is called for.

The specific performance measures used to evaluate performance are, of necessity, determined by the team's goal. They might be achievement of the team's planned tasks or business goals, customer satisfaction, production costs, product quality, delivery time, or profitability. Indeed, traditional performance evaluation is most often oriented toward results or output. But while results are still critical, the *way* in which the team achieves those results is also important. You might call these "process factors." They are particularly important for interim performance evaluations when *how* the team is working together is a likely predictor of its ultimate success or failure. Process factors—both for individuals and the team as a whole—include:

- Commitment to team work

- The level of individual participation and individual leadership

- Oral and written communication within and on behalf of the team

- Collaboration

- Conflict resolution

- Planning and goal setting

- Win-win decision making

- Problem solving and application of analytical skills

- Level of credibility and trust

- Adherence to agreed-upon processes and procedures

- Application of project-management skills (e.g., budgeting and scheduling)

- Building and sustaining interpersonal relationships

- Willingness to change and take risks

- Individual and team learning

Evaluation Methods

Once you've determined the basis on which performance will be evaluated, give some thought to the method. There are many different approaches available for measuring your team's success. They vary widely in complexity, cost, and time required. Consider a more elaborate method for a team whose mission is extensive and will have a significant impact on organizational performance; for teams with narrower missions, simpler methods generally work well. The methods include:

- Benchmarking against similar teams in other organizations. This can be costly and time-consuming—and there may be no comparable teams to be found.

- Evaluating the team's progress against original goals and schedules. This may be the gold standard, given that goals are the focus of all team effort. The schedule may be less important, and for two reasons. First, the team may be behind schedule owing to factors beyond its control. Second, every team project is susceptible to surprises and the discovery of new opportunities. Holding people too tightly to an arbitrary schedule set down in the first weeks of a project will discourage people from pursuing the opportunities they discover in the course of their work.

- Observation of the team by an outside consultant. Enlisting the help of a neutral party is a good way to obtain an objective evaluation. And if the consultant has experience in the area of the team's mission, he or she will be in a position to compare team performance against similar teams working elsewhere (i.e., benchmarking).

- Encouraging regular, informal team discussions to assess the team's functioning. Such meetings are perfectly adequate for a short-duration project team.

- Project debriefing sessions to identify what did and did not go well and how this learning can help future projects. These opportunities are an excellent way to evaluate performance *and* help members face up to what they are doing well and doing wrong.

Evaluation of Individual Team Members

Team members perform a number of roles—for example, as individual contributors, as members of the team, and as members of the larger organization. Thus, in reviewing performance, it is helpful to combine at least a couple of the following methods to address performance in each of those roles:

- **Peer rating.** Team members assess each other's contributions.

- **Customer satisfaction rating.** Internal and external customers rate the performance of the team and of its individual members.

- **Self-appraisal.** Each team member rates his or her own performance.

- **Team leader review.** You, as the team leader or the supervisor, evaluate each individual's performance.

- **Management review.** Department heads or managers of the team leaders evaluate individual and team performance.

None of those methods is perfect, which is why combining the results of several can give you and team members a more complete read of their performance.

Summing Up

- Once you've launched a team effort, pay close attention to the processes through which members collaborate, share information, and get the job done. Dysfunctional processes will cause the team to fail.

- As you monitor collaboration, watch out for any member who tries to take undue credit for team-based work, who is always pressing for a larger share of resources, or who is secretive.

- Encourage team members to share information; encourage departments with important data to share relevant data with the team.

- If an individual creates conflict within the team, there are two approaches to dealing with it: open team discussion and discussion through private channels.

- To maintain momentum and keep motivation high, break tasks into manageable pieces.

- Celebrate each milestone as it is accomplished.

- Teams learn to work better together. Support rapid learning by (1) selecting team members who are eager to learn, (2) getting people to focus on the lessons they learn from their experience, and (3) giving people opportunities to experiment.

- Be a learning leader. Be accessible, ask for input, and admit your mistakes.

- When you evaluate team performance, don't focus exclusively on results, particularly in the early stages. Give equal attention to "process factors."

The Virtual Team

A Collaborative Challenge

Key Topics Covered in This Chapter

- *What can be gained from virtual teams—and why they can be more difficult to manage*

- *The technology available for virtual team communications*

- *Making decisions about technology*

- *How to manage the main challenges of virtual teams: team identity, commitment, and collaboration*

- *Coaching the virtual team*

THE TERM *virtual team* refers to a team that, for the most part, is linked through communication that is not face to face: e-mail, voice mail, telephone, groupware, videoconferencing. Many of today's teams are virtual to some extent—that is, they include members who are physically separated from their teammates: company employees in distant locations, employees of alliance partners, a representative of a key supplier, or perhaps an important customer. Some teams are entirely virtual; their members rarely if ever meet face-to-face. Nevertheless, virtual teams are real teams, and many have performed their missions very well. This chapter begins with the benefits of virtual teams and then moves on to the challenges they present to team leaders and members.[1]

Benefits and Challenges

Virtual teams provide substantial opportunities to organizations in both the public and private sectors. With virtual teams working literally around the world, a company can stay open twenty-four hours a day. Its customer service personnel can respond to customer demands around the clock. Such teams are a natural and convenient way to work closely with customers. Product design teams can also work around the clock. For example, at quitting time in Hamburg, the German members of a virtual team can forward the result of their day's work to their U.S. colleagues based in Connecticut; those members will begin their day where the Germans left off, eventually forwarding the output of their day's work to another group in

Sydney, Australia. Like relay racers, these team members keep the baton moving forward.

Virtual teams also make it easier to bring together a more diverse group of skills, experiences, and knowledge about customers, supplier contacts, and interests than would otherwise be possible. Consider this example:

> *A team of product developers is working on a new electronic household appliance aimed at a worldwide market. By design, its team members are based in North America, Europe, and Asia and are native to those regions. This arrangement strengthens the team's ability to recognize and accommodate customer tastes and product uses, and to incorporate the safety and electrical standards of different countries.*

The cultural diversity represented on this virtual team enhances its potential to accomplish great things—things that might be impossible if approached through a traditional team collocated in a single R&D facility.

Virtual teams present many challenges to leaders and members. People who organize such teams must, like traditional team leaders, be concerned about clarity of goals, bringing together the right set of skills, gaining member commitment, and so forth. They must also ensure adequate collaboration and information sharing and create rewards that align effort with team goals. These principles of team building are essentially the same. So what is different? What are the unique challenges to team management and effectiveness?

Virtual teams present two unique challenges. The first is a management problem: How do you apply what you know about managing teams to virtual work? The other problem is technological: What tools do you need to keep team members connected, communicating, and collaborating? Let's consider the technical issues first.

Virtual Team Technology

A virtual team depends on technology. Can you imagine a cross-border team accomplishing anything in an era before e-mail, the Internet, and international phone service? Technology provides the linkages through which participants can share ideas and information, coordinate activities, and build bonds of trust. Neither the leader nor the members need be technology experts, but they must be prepared to use or learn the technology that's required to do the job.

Some basic technology is necessary for every virtual team. Everyone will need telephones, e-mail, Internet access, and, possibly, access to fax machines. Beyond these, other technologies can help team members communicate and work together.

E–Mail

Everyone on a virtual team needs an e-mail address. If you plan to rely heavily on e-mailing attached documents, check for compatibility and compression issues with each team member, and establish protocols for use. Everyone on the team should know when, why, and to whom to send e-mails. Be clear about who must be "copied" on what, and don't overdo it. There's probably no need to "cc" every person on the team list with every correspondence you send out. Nobody wants to receive massive amounts of irrelevant e-mail. But make sure that everyone is informed about decisions that affect

---

Enforce E-Mail Security

E-mail is a helpful and time-saving device. But beware of the following two security issues:

1. E-mail is often read by more people than their senders intended. A recipient will often forward an e-mail to many others without thinking about the consequences of sharing the information it contains.

2. Erasing e-mail from your hard drive does not eliminate it. Investigators and practitioners of industrial espionage have software capable of retrieving deleted messages and their attachments. So do not include sensitive or confidential information in an e-mail.

them, and make sure that the people who need to participate in decisions are consulted.

E-mails create virtual paper trails that can be important down the line if misunderstandings or conflicts arise.

Web and Intranet Sites

The Web has changed the way virtual teams work. A project Web site can substitute for the team room. Using browsers they already have, members can go to a project Web site to review posted deliverables, to check schedules, and to get information. *Intranet* sites—that is, private corporate networks that use standard Internet protocols—can work in much the same way.

A virtual team room can be set up in the project Web site using four walls, like those in a real team room:

- **Purpose wall.** This wall includes the team charter, goals, tasks, a list of deliverables, and current results.

- **People wall.** This section identifies the team members and states their roles. Here, users can find out who is involved with different aspects of the project. If possible, attach a photo of each team member and a brief description of his or her particular work and expertise. Putting a face and a bit of history with a name adds an important dimension to virtual team work.

- **Document wall.** This part of the site contains a schedule of upcoming meetings and their agendas. Minutes of past meetings and any meeting presentations are also stored on this wall. Members can use this wall to post their work for review by colleagues. Those reviews and comments can likewise be posted.

- **Communications wall.** This section contains links and information that connect everyone on the team.

Web sites are great assets, but they require some tending. Someone must monitor and update the site. Depending on the scope of the project, this important job could be someone's total contribution to the team.

Groupware

Groupware describes software applications that help people work together. More specifically, groupware is integrative software that allows users operating from different workstations to communicate concurrently. Examples include Livelink, Lotus Notes, Novell Group-Wise, Oracle, and others.

Groupware is useful to virtual teams because it provides access to databases and support for virtual meetings. Some groupware can be used for "live" meetings in which people work online and on the phone at the same time. It can be used for e-mail, discussion groups, and bulletin boards. Groupware allows access to shared databases and applications, calendars and scheduling, and reference libraries. Some packages include support for voice conferencing and electronic whiteboards.

But groupware is not essential. It is less expensive to establish a group Web or intranet site than it is to purchase groupware for all participants because team members only need a browser. And you won't have to deal with the compatibility problems that often occur with groupware.

Database Access

Databases contain documents and other information that's useful to the team. They are accessible from Web sites, from intranet sites, and through groupware. Documents in databases often contain sensitive material. Some virtual team members may be allowed to change such documents, but your organization may want to restrict that capability. For example, nonemployee team members like customers or vendors may have access to view restricted documents but may not be able to edit them.

Fax Machines

The dedicated fax machine is on its way out as a mode of communication. Many of its functions can be done more easily through e-mail. Even documents, newspaper clippings, photos, and so forth can be sent as e-mail attachments if they are scanned into files. But since many people do not have easy access to scanners and scanning can take time, fax machines continue to serve a useful purpose.

Text–Editing Software

Teams are forever generating and submitting reports. Since several members must collaborate in report development, they need a handy way of incorporating changes into electronic files. Chances are, the word processors used in your organization have a feature that allows users to track changes made in a document. Few people are even aware of this feature. Fewer still have any experience in using it.

Here's how the track–changes feature works. Deleted text is crossed out but is still visible on the screen. Newly added text is in color (with different colors for different reviewers), and marks in the margins make changes easy to spot. This function provides a quick and precise way for many people to review and contribute to a document. And if a document is saved before revisions are accepted, collaborators will have a permanent record of what was changed and who made the changes. For example:

Helen has accepted the job of writing a progress report for her team. Maurice and Lynn have agreed to review her draft and offer suggestions. Before computers were prevalent, Helen would have sent her draft as a paper document to her collaborators, who would have scratched out words or phrases they didn't like and suggested additions in the margins. The marked-up copies would have been returned to Helen by mail or fax, who would have incorporated all changes into a final draft.

Thanks to the editing feature in her word-processing software, Helen can get the job done faster and easier. She sent her draft as an e-mail attachment to Maurice with this message: "Please indicate what changes are needed and then forward it on to Lynn for her input. Feel free to add material where necessary. Just be sure to turn on the track-changes feature before you begin editing."

When she receives the edited document from her collaborators, Helen will be able to see all the changes and additions. Maurice's work will be in red and Lynn's in blue. If Helen finds a change in

---

Watch Out for Compatibility Problems

Some people think that their technology is compatible because they're using the same software and the same computers. But they may have unexpected problems "unstuffing" compressed files. And file compression is commonplace when people are sending big PowerPoint and similar files via e-mail. Run tests to determine whether any of your team members have compatibility problems. You may need to have all teammates install a common file-compression program.

---

blue that she doesn't agree with, she'll call Lynn on the phone to discuss their differences.

Once all changes have been reviewed and discussed with the collaborators, Helen will accept the changes. Her report will then incorporate her material as well as improvements made by her teammates.

Text-revision features do not solve the problems that go hand-in-hand with committee-written material, but it makes the collaboration process easier to handle.

Meeting Technology

There are times when e-mails won't do—when team members simply must get together to talk about their work. In some cases, the ability to communicate verbally is sufficient. In others, people must also be able to see each other or the physical objects that others are working on: a person who has just joined the team, a product prototype, or different color choices for a new product. Sometimes they may want to speak directly with a customer about how he has adapted the team's product to make it more effective.

TELEPHONE CONFERENCING. The telephone conference is the quickest and easiest way for the virtual team to communicate verbally. A telephone conference is often necessary to review key deliverables, to discuss strategy, and to brainstorm. Many kinds of technologies exist, from built-in conferencing in telephone systems to conferences hosted by communication service providers.

VIDEOCONFERENCING. Videoconferencing is another channel of team connectivity. It can bring teams together without wasting time or money spent on meals, travel, and lodging. Team members located in London, for example, can see and interact with their colleagues in Rome without leaving their offices. Videoconferencing, however, is complicated and requires the help of people with specialized technical skills. For basic video, each participant needs the appropriate computer, camera, microphone, software, and Internet connection. Unfortunately, systems from different vendors aren't always compatible with different computers, so if your team opts for video, be sure everyone gets a compatible system.

Visual Trumps Audio

In their valuable article "Distance Matters," Gary Olson and Judith Olson conclude that attempts to use connective technologies either fail or require major efforts by team members to adjust to using the media technologies. Apart from that blanket conclusion, they note that video connections are far superior to audio alone:

Our laboratory data show that even for people who know each other and have worked together before, a simple audio connection for conversation and a shared editor for real-time work is insufficient to produce the same quality of work as that done face-to-face. Those with video connections produced output that was indistinguishable from that produced by people who were face to face. The process of their work changed, however, to require more clarification and more management overhead (discussions about how they will conduct the work, not actually doing the work).

SOURCE: Gary M. Olson and Judith S. Olson, "Distance Matters," *Human Computer Interactions*, 15 (2000): 152.

WHITEBOARDS. An electronic whiteboard makes it possible for team members to see a drawing or chart on their PCs. For instance, if a team leader in Houston, Texas, draws a new product on an electronic whiteboard, the rest of the team will be able to see the image on their computer screens. If they are also connected through teleconferencing, team members will be able to discuss the sketch and recommend changes—and all in real time. If you can't make a point without a marker in your hand, investigate conferencing options that include whiteboard support.

Making Technology Decisions

Common sense, the team's combined knowledge, and expert help from your organization's IT department can help you find the most appropriate technology for your purposes. So too can the following who, what, when, and how questions:

- **Who?** Who's on the team? Are they technology-ready? Knowing who's on the team and how they relate to technology will give you a realistic idea of what you can expect them to do with technology, and how long it might take them to get up to speed. If your team members are novices and not particularly keen on taking the time to become more tech-savvy, stick with the simple and the familiar.

- **What?** What do you need to do? What is the nature of the team's work? What software do you currently use? What compatibility issues are involved? What information do you work with now? What is the most common technology platform in the organization? What are your communications needs? Answering what questions will help you plan for new technology or upgrades before the project gets under way.

- **When?** When is your team project scheduled to begin and end? Acquiring and installing new technology takes time, and still more time is needed to train people in its use.

- **Where?** Where will you be when you send or receive information? From where will others send information? Where will it

A Caveat on Connective Technology

The connective technologies described in this chapter may be just what your widely scattered team needs to communicate, co-ordinate, and share ideas and information. But if you have team members in developing countries, you may have a problem. Some of these countries do not have reliable or secure Internet service providers. Others lack reliable phone service. And many have off-again, on-again electrical power. So before you leap on board with any of the latest connective technologies, consider the supportive infrastructures in the countries where your team members are located.

be received? Where is the information you'll need? Track the desired flow of information—where it will come from and where it should go. Answer those questions, and you'll be better prepared to design an information system that suits your needs.

- **How?** How can you best use what you have? How flexible do you need to be? How much can you afford to spend? Analyze the possibilities of using what you have. Adapting it to your needs will probably be the cheapest course to follow and may make it easier for team members to master the technology. Anticipate technology needs that may come up during the course of the project. Determine how flexible you will need to be, and try to build in technology solutions today that can be adapted to your needs tomorrow.

Managing the Virtual Team

Managing is the second major challenge of virtual teams. As one team of researchers has noted, "Differences in local physical context, time zones, culture, and language all persist."[2] Even with the application of connective technology, the fundamental concerns of team management—team identity, commitment, and collaboration—

become even more pronounced. We addressed those issues earlier in this book. They need to be revisited, however, in context of the virtual team.

Team Identity

Individuals who identify with a team or a group generally exhibit the behaviors that form the bedrock of team success; they work harder, collaborate more fully, and, in many cases, put the interests of the team ahead of their own. Identity with a group usually goes hand in hand with trust, which, in turn, encourages information sharing and collaboration.

Team identity doesn't happen naturally in virtual teams, and for obvious reasons. If the team and its members are out of sight, they are also out of mind. In the worst cases, the virtual team is a collection of strangers with few, if any, social bonds. As you can probably imagine, it is very difficult to develop a sense of identity with a group of people you seldom see. But there are things you can do:

- **Hold a launch meeting.** If possible, gather everyone together for this meeting—even if it is the only time they will rub shoulders during the course of the team project. While they are together, create opportunities for members to get acquainted on a personal level. The idea is to create small-group cohesion. If the group is small, for example, introduce each member and ask him or her to say something about his or her background, special skills, hobbies, personal interests, and so forth.

  Over the course of the one- or two-day launch meeting, assign people to subgroups, each charged with discussing a particular facet of the task. Rotate people in these subgroups so that everyone gets a chance to meet and work with everyone else. At the end of your launch meeting, take a group picture, and send copies to all participants.

- **Encourage periodic face-to-face meetings as the work progresses**. If the team is not too broadly dispersed—and if the budget permits—bring people together again at key junctures (e.g., when commitment must be renewed, when several new members have joined the team, when key decisions must be made, or when the next phase of the project must be planned and assigned). Use videoconferencing if physical meetings are not feasible. Doing so will reinforce the group bonding that occurred at the team launch. If you cannot bring the entire team together, do so for important subgroups.

- **Find times when people can get together.** This is bound to be difficult for teams that span continents and time zones, so schedule regular meeting times for conference calls or Internet chats, and arrange a process to discuss concerns about the project. This will help team members feel comfortable sharing thoughts and will promote a team approach instead of encourage people to work individually.

  One warning: If the company headquarters is in the United States, don't arrange things so that the Asian or Australian team members must always take calls in the middle of the night, during regular U.S. business hours. Doing so will annoy your partners on the other side of the globe and make them feel like second-class teammates. Pass this hardship around equally.

- **Form team identity around goals.** Just as raindrops form around bits of atmospheric dust, team identity needs something solid to form around. You should use team goals for this purpose.

Commitment

Commitment to the team and its goals is a must-have for success. If they lack commitment, members will allocate their energy and time to other goals; they will participate only to the extent that their schedules permit. People will only commit to things that they see as being very important—either important projects overall or important to their careers.

The most practical approach to obtaining commitment within a virtual team is to be very selective about who is invited to join it. Within the constraint of required skills, leaders should pick people who have strong, natural interests in the team's goals, as in this example:

Frank was appointed to lead a virtual team to develop environmentally friendly standards for the company's product packaging. His boss put it to him this way: "Times are changing, Frank. People are beginning to resist excessive packaging, including ours. They aren't interested in paying for cardboard and plastic that will end up in a landfill."

As Frank thought about the right people for his team, his thoughts turned to Agnes, who conducted focus-group research for the marketing department. She understood the people who bought the company's products. Best of all, Agnes was keenly interested in environmental issues. In fact, she had once encouraged the new-product group to design environmentally damaging materials out of all company products. "Some other manufacturers are doing this," she told them. "They're saving money and generating goodwill with their customers as a result." She would have a strong natural commitment to the team's goal.

If you follow that example, just be sure that the people you invite to join the team bring something in addition to a strong personal interest in team goals. They should also bring important skills to the effort.

Collaboration

The whole point of a team is to get people with complementary capabilities to work *together* on important tasks. It's the union of complementary skills that gives teams the power that traditional work groups lack. But is collaboration possible between virtual team members? If it is, what is the basis for collaboration, and how can it be encouraged?

Yes, collaboration is possible. Here are a few tips for getting more of it:

- Create opportunities for collaboration. You can do this with the kinds of communication tools described above. Communication lubricates the wheels of collaboration.

- Recognize and praise collaborative behavior when you see it. Broadcast the fact that two team members are making progress on the team's presentation to management. Announce via e-mail the market-research piece developed by Hal in New Orleans and Jennifer in Miami.

Do a Culture Check

If you're working with a global virtual team, especially with new members, do a culture check. How do these team members feel about working conditions, hours, authority and delegation, communication patterns (especially what is considered polite or not), and other culturally determined activities? For example, in some countries, a manager loses respect if he or she does not maintain a very formal relationship with subordinates. In other countries, formality is not valued. The team leader caught in the middle of these disparate attitudes and customs must recognize them and tread with caution. Even the act of praising someone for a job well done can backfire on a team leader who is not aware of cultural differences. The notion of singling out individuals for praise in front of others is normal in North America but a source of embarrassment and discomfort for the affected team member who happens to be from a culture that places its emphasis on groups.

Get the Specifications Right

Communication is usually the greatest impediment for cross-cultural teams. Not every team member will have total mastery of the language in which people agree to communicate. And this can lead to misunderstandings.

Writing in the *Harvard Management Communications Letter,* Kim Ribbink describes how one U.S. corporate manager has reduced the chance of miscommunication with technical workers for whom English is a second language. This manager implemented a policy under which any project specifications he assigns are "reverse-specified" by the assignee. In other words, the assignee will write the assignment's specifications as he or she understands them. Those specs are then discussed with the manager to eliminate any conflicts or misunderstandings. This way, everyone is clear about the requirements and what the results should be.

SOURCE: Kim Ribbink, "Seven Ways to Better Communicate in Today's Diverse Workplace," *Harvard Management Communication Letter,* November 2002.

Normal work hours is another important issue. As mentioned earlier, be respectful of the fact that your conference calls may force team members in other time zones to work either very late in the evening or before the crack of dawn. Are such requirements acceptable in those cultures? Will those team members accept such hours if they are tied to that schedule over a long period of time? What weekend work, holiday work, and overtime do people expect? Those questions need to be carefully considered and discussed with all members of the team.

The cross-cultural team must also agree on issues of language and measures. In what language (or languages) will discussion and reporting be made? Will budgets be expressed in U.S. dollars, in euros, or in some other currency? Will the team describe all specifications in the Anglo-American systems of inches, pounds, and ounces or in the more generally accepted metric measures?

Coaching the Team You Can't See

In a traditional team, performance can usually be improved through coaching. And there are many opportunities for doing so: One member doesn't know how to work with others; another member must develop a PowerPoint presentation but hasn't ever used the program; yet another is having trouble balancing her regular departmental duties with her team duties. In each instance, the team leader should do some coaching—or enlist another qualified person to do the job.

The virtual team has similar opportunities for coaching, but getting the job done is more difficult. With members scattered in different locations and different time zones, the communications required for effective coaching are less available. The team leader cannot simply walk over to the other person's office and demonstrate how to use presentation software or to set up a budget report.

A little analysis of peoples' schedules and a dose of planning, however, can overcome some problems of distance. Virtual team leaders can, for example, schedule weekly or daily conference calls to keep the doors of communication open. They can set intersecting office hours when people will be available for team work and phone calls—times that do not infringe on members' nonteam obligations. So do the following:

- Let people know when it's okay to call each other.

- Have team members set regular times daily when they are available for mutual team work and communication. (Work out compromises for different time zones and sleep habits.)

- Make a rule to respect agreed-upon hours for communication.

Every performance problem has a source, and it's the coach's job to find it. If a team member is missing deadlines or falling behind, for example, contact the person and ask why. If distractions are getting in the way, find out the source of the distractions. Ask what you can do to help. If the person appears to be overwhelmed by his or her assignment, break the large task into smaller tasks and try to farm some of them out to other team members who have extra time.

Tips for Getting a Virtual Team Off to a Good Start

The importance of a launch meeting has already been mentioned. Here are other things that will set your virtual team on a path that leads to success.

- **Provide a clear vision and workable goals at the very beginning.** Without these, a virtual team will quickly run off the tracks. Like all teams, a virtual one must examine its objectives and make adjustments during the course of its work. Nevertheless, it should spend substantial time in the beginning on mapping out the vision and goals.

- **Clarify roles.** All team members should know what they are supposed to be doing. A virtual team stands no chance of success if roles are not clearly defined from the beginning.

Continued

Without the water-cooler conferences, chats at the cube, casual lunches, or five-minute stand-up meetings that benefit a same-place team, the virtual team has far fewer opportunities to answer the question "Who's doing what?"

- **Stay organized.** The leader or project manager should create a work plan and sustain the multiple long-distance relationships during the course of the project. Although such tasks are required of any leader, it is particularly important for a virtual team leader to be well organized, because the chances of things falling through the cracks are so much greater.

- **Be clear on key questions.** Everyone on the team must participate in a process that defines the following:

  What are we doing and when?

  Who is responsible and accountable?

  How do we do it?

  How will we know when it's done?

  How will we (and others) monitor progress and performance?

  How will we (and others) measure results?

Summing Up

- Virtual teams offer the potential of working around the clock, harnessing diverse skills, and bringing many varied perspectives to a problem or project.

- Like traditional teams, virtual teams must have clarity about their goals, bring together the right set of skills, gain the commitment of their members, develop a team identity that is associated with mutual accountability, and support team efforts with appropriate rewards.

- Virtual teams present two unique challenges: managing collaboration and progress by dispersed members, and keeping members connected and in communication with one another.

- Communications technologies can help virtual teams stay connected. These include e-mail, faxes, phone conferencing, videoconferencing, Web sites, and groupware.

- Web sites are ideal cyberspace locations for creating virtual team rooms, document libraries, and meeting schedules.

- Team identity—an important issue for every team—is even more challenging for virtual teams. Leaders can build team identity by holding a launch meeting and periodic face-to-face gatherings, by establishing regular communications, and by focusing on team goals.

- Team leaders and members must be particularly sensitive to cultural differences among members.

- As with a traditional team, coaching can improve the performance of virtual teams.

8

Becoming a Team Player

Your Most Important Assignment

Key Topics Covered in This Chapter

- *Why being open to new ideas can produce synergy within the team*

- *How different ways of working are expected by team players*

- *Seeking alternative solutions*

- *Tips for developing working relationships with people from different functions*

- *Finding win-win solutions*

- *Why you should avoid teams whose goals you do not value highly*

- *Guidelines for being a reliable teammate*

- *The importance of being results-oriented*

TEAM PERFORMANCE is only as strong as the collective performance of its members. At a minimum, performance should be the sum of the individual efforts of team members and leaders. In a four-person team that would look like this: $1 + 1 + 1 + 1 = 4$. Some teams unfortunately experience "process loss"—that is, their total performance is something less than the sum of their individual contributors. These teams are wasteful and inefficient.

When individuals behave like team players instead of solo performers, however, collective output increases to something like this: $1 + 1 + 1 + 1 = 5$. While that equation makes no mathematical sense, it is made possible by the synergistic effects of bringing together collaborative people with complementary skills. It is the same synergistic effect created when a company with a great new product merges with another company that has a powerful distribution system. As stand-alone enterprises, each would turn in an average performance. Put them together and great things happen.

Your team can get the same synergistic performance benefit, but only if its members behave like team players. What does it mean to be a team player? A team player is committed, collaborative, and competent. We've discussed those characteristics in previous chapters. This chapter suggests specific, less obvious things you can do to become a better team player.

Be Open to New Ideas

Teams are miniature societies in which strains of thinking from different sources and disciplines bump up against each other. The marketing person on a bank's team for new products and services, for instance, is outward-looking by training and habit. Anytime a new service or product is proposed, he automatically thinks about how the bank's current customers would respond to it. "What about prospective new customers?" he asks. "Given this product's price and features, will customers perceive it as a good value? How will it stack up against our competitors' services?" His mind is always in the external world of customers, markets, and business rivals. That thinking is automatic for a person with a marketing background.

The team's financial specialist, on the other hand, will immediately focus on costs, revenues, and profitability when new services are discussed. He asks, "What will be the fixed and variable costs of each unit of service we produce? Is marketing's estimate of first-year revenue conservative or optimistic? What will be the breakeven point for profitability?"

For her part, the operations person on the team is largely concerned with the work processes through which the new service will be produced. "What would be the most efficient way to provide this service?" she ponders. "How long will it take to staff and train the people we'd need? Where could we speed up the process and reduce labor through software?"

Each of the three employees in this example is working on the same new banking service team. Each brings a very different set of knowledge, experience, and concerns to the endeavor. And each is concentrating on one aspect of a multifaceted problem. It's very possible that they can loosely cobble their perspectives together to produce an appealing new and profitable banking service. It could happen. But think for a moment about how much more likely their success would be if they could seamlessly combine their separate perspectives. For instance, if the operations person understood more about customer preferences and more about the financial specialist's concerns, she might develop an insight:

If most customers are already knowledgeable about this type of financial service and are most likely to purchase it outside normal business hours, we should provide the bulk of it through self-service on our home-banking Web site. That would shift our cost from mostly variable to mostly fixed —that is, for software development—costs. Our breakeven point for profitability would definitely go up as a result, but once we passed that point, most revenues would fall directly to the profitability line.

The melding of the different perspectives and ideas demonstrated in that example gives teams real power. You can contribute to that power by being open to new ideas and different ways of thinking. Try this:

- Make a genuine effort to understand and respect the different viewpoints represented on the team. One of them may contain a hidden gold mine.

- Don't be too quick to dismiss new ideas. Instead, adopt a position of scientific skepticism. Ask people to back up their ideas with data and rational argument. For example, instead of saying "That won't work," say something like this: "That's an interesting idea, Fred, but I don't understand how it could work, given what that approach would probably cost. Could you explain it in greater detail and tell us your cost estimate?"

Following these tips will make you a better team player.

Be Open to Different Ways of Working

Most of us do almost all of our work within our home departments. That work gets to be very routine after a while. Managers and consultants have probably spent lots of time developing a machinelike routine, and they expect us to follow it. Self-managed work teams likewise develop routines and stick to them, making incremental improvements here and there.

When you're thrown into a cross-functional project team, however, your routine way of working disappears. Suddenly, you are making up the work from scratch and doing things you generally don't do: planning a four-month project, working with people on a budget, being assigned to a new and unfamiliar role, working closely with people with very different skills and experiences than your own. If you are a manager, you find that yours is just one voice among many; the authority you normally have is now shared with others. Some people find these types of change refreshing, but many others do not. For them, diversions from routines and existing workplace patterns create tension, anxiety, discomfort, and even fear.

Being a good team player requires that you develop some comfort with these changes and with different ways of working. So relax. They are not going to kill you. Try to do the following:

- Approach new ways of working with a positive attitude. Look for things you can learn that will improve your performance when you return to your regular job. Think of how mastery of these new working methods will make you more valuable and employable.

- Be open-minded about different ways of tackling team tasks, recognizing better ways of working when you see them.

- Look for opportunities to collaborate where doing so would produce the greatest synergy.

Share What You Have

There's an old saying that from those to whom much has been given, much is expected. So when you join a team, be prepared to share what you have and what you know—including information, experience, and specialized know-how. You were, after all, selected for the team because of your skills and expertise. People will naturally look to you for those unique qualities, just as you will look to others to share their special qualities. Be prepared to do so through the following:

- Teaching—For example, if you are familiar with the groupware the team plans to use, provide a tutorial for teammates who have never used it.

- Providing relevant information—If you are the marketing person on the team, disclose what your department has learned about customers and competitors.

Seek Alternatives

There is a certain amount of flailing around during the early days of a team effort. The team has been chartered with an end, but the means must be determined through discussion. In the course of that discussion, alternative sets of tasks and courses of action are routinely proposed and debated. Most people approach these debates with the understanding that they must support one alternative or another. Don't make that mistake. Instead, use this initial period to expand the set of feasible alternatives. Consider this example:

> *Andrea was recruited to a management team whose goal was to determine how best to deal with a piece of vacant land owned by her company that's directly adjacent to its current headquarters building. As senior management framed the problem, there were two alternatives: (a) sell the land, or (b) expand the current building onto it. Management wanted the team to investigate the best option for the company.*
>
> *The team's charter, as Andrea saw clearly, was not to choose between a and b, but to investigate the best option for the company. So she quickly set about expanding the set of alternative opinions, looking into building on the site, leasing the space, and so forth. Each of the alternatives was then analyzed to determine which represented the greatest value to the company.*

In expanding the set of alternatives, Andrea was acting as a team player. But acknowledging the possibilities available to the team is only half the battle. Objective analysis of each choice is the second half. In some cases, the features of different alternatives can be combined into a superior hybrid version.

Develop Working Relationships with People from Different Functions

People trained in different specialized areas don't always work well together—at least not at first. Harvard Business School Professor Morten Hansen has pointed to a "chemistry problem" that often prevents people from working effectively with others, even when they know that collaboration is essential. In his view, this problem often results from people not knowing each other and not having experience collaborating with each other. He cites a study of time-to-market performance of new-product-development projects in a high-technology company that found that "project engineers who worked with engineers from other divisions took 20 to 30 percent longer to complete their projects when they had not established a personal relationship. Engineers found it hard to articulate, understand, and absorb complex technologies that were transferred between divisions when they had not learned to work together beforehand."[1] Fortunately, antidotes to the problem cited by Hansen are available:

- Bring in a training coach or facilitator. They specialize in developing collaborative behavior in groups.

- Get to know every team member with whom you'll have contact. Get to know these individuals at both professional and personal levels. You don't have to like them or be their friend, but you do need to understand how they think and what motivates and engages their best work. Once you are acquainted, communication between you will be easier and more effective.

- If possible, reduce the risks in initial collaborations by beginning with the least difficult tasks. You can develop a positive chemistry with others by simply working on tasks together. Move on to more challenging tasks once the chemistry has developed.

Look for Win–Win Solutions

Being a team player doesn't mean that you have to give in on things that matter to you and let other people get their way. A little creativity and good negotiating skills can often recast a win-lose situation into one in which all parties can be satisfied.

If you're over fifty, you probably remember the insistence that you can either have high quality or low cost; you can't have both. That theory was eventually proved false. The quality movement that emerged in the 1970s showed the marketplace that high quality and low cost were not mutually exclusive. Both values could be captured. It's not hard to find analogous situations in team settings, where divergent interests are generally in play. People who are not team players see debates as win-lose and try to position themselves on the winning side. Their gain, of course, disadvantages their teammates, creating resentment and undermining future collaboration. Real team players approach conflicts more carefully. They consider the interests of the different parties and then try to find a solution that will create value for both.

Finding opportunities for mutual benefit requires information sharing. Unlike the win-lose mentality that encourages people to play their cards close to the vest, a win-win mentality encourages people to be very open—that is,

- provide significant information about their circumstances,

- talk about their real interests, and

- reveal and explain their preferences among options.

Breakthroughs like these require trust between the different parties. If they lack that trust, each group fears that any revelation of important information will be used against it. Trust isn't always there in the beginning, but it grows as people get to know each other and enjoy some success in working together.

As you negotiate with other people, don't feel that you must compromise on issues that are important to you. Compromising is easy to do, and it relieves the impasses caused by disagreement.

However, compromising on things that matter—quality, customer requirements, design, and so forth—can also lead to second-rate results. So instead of finding middle ground every time you and your teammates disagree, look for trade-offs that will satisfy the other side's interests *without* conceding on the issues you think are very important.

Only Join Teams Whose Goals You Value Highly

Earlier in this book, commitment was cited as essential for team success. Every member—including you—must be committed to the same goal. You're unlikely to muster real commitment, however, if you don't view the team's goals as particularly valuable. And if you don't, you'll find excuses to spend your time on other duties. You won't be a good team player. Conversely, if team values and your personal values are aligned, you will do whatever it takes to move the team toward its objectives. As author John Maxwell has written: "Anytime you make choices based on solid life values, then you're in a better position to sustain your level of commitment because you don't have to continually reevaluate its importance. . . . A commitment to something you believe in is a commitment that is easier to keep."[2] If you're considering joining a team or if someone is trying to volunteer you for team duty, keep these points in mind:

- Consider your commitment level. You'll be a half-baked team player if you are not fully committed to the team's goals.

- Check your level of enthusiasm before joining a team. Unless you're enthusiastic, you won't give it your all.

Be a Reliable Teammate

People like to work with reliable teammates. Dependable individuals can be trusted to do their share of the work, do it well, and get it done on time. They do what they say they'll do. When the going gets tough, their help can be counted on. To be a reliable partner, follow these guidelines:

- Only make promises you intend to keep.

- Never commit to tasks you cannot complete.

- Be prepared and on time for meetings; finish work on schedule.

- Deliver only good work.

- Make your word your bond.

- Be frank and objective when people ask for an evaluation.

Be Results-Oriented

Many teams make the mistake of focusing too much on training, planning, and preparation and too little on producing results. Those early-stage activities are important—even essential. But they should not deflect attention from the team's real purpose: to produce results. Per Robert Schaffer and Harvey Thomson's research, training, planning, and preparation "sound good, look good, and allow managers to feel good," but beyond some point they no longer contribute to bottom-line performance.[3] The researchers cite the example of one major enterprise that, after three years, proudly pointed to forty-eight improvement teams, high morale, and two completed quality-improvement plans—but absolutely *no* measurable performance improvement!

Some team members find satisfaction in attending meetings, expressing their views on what should be done, and developing plans. But they never get around to doing anything that produces tangible results. Don't be that type of team player. Yes, meetings and planning are necessary, but don't let them become your focus. Concentrate instead on producing results. Doing so will be easier if you:

- Set a series of short-term goals and pursue them one by one.

- End every meeting with a set of action assignments—and then complete your assignments.

- If your team includes members who are long on talking and short on doing, make them uncomfortable. If one of them suggests, "Somebody should test that idea on current and prospective customers," give this response: "That's a good idea, how soon can you complete that test and give us the result?" With luck, they'll leave the team.

Are you a good team player? Are you reliable and effective? This chapter has identified and explained things you can do to become the kind of teammate that others will respect and look forward to working with. This book has covered all the essential topics of effective teams and team management. But in the end, knowing how to become a good team player may be the most important.

Summing Up

- If you want to be a team player, be open to new ideas and different ways of working. Approach them with a positive attitude.

- Share your information, experience, and specialized know-how.

- Don't be satisfied with the obvious options or courses of action facing your team. Instead, seek feasible alternatives. When possible, combine the best features of various options to create superior alternatives.

- When you work with new teammates, try to begin with easy tasks. You can develop a positive chemistry with others by simply working on tasks together.

- Team-based work involves negotiating. Avoid win-lose negotiations in favor of those from which all parties can obtain value. Mutual trust and a willingness to share information and reveal one's own interests are the basis for win-win negotiations.

- You're unlike to muster real commitment if you don't view the team's goals as particularly valuable.

- If you want to be a good team player, be a reliable partner. Make only those promises you intend to keep, be prompt, and deliver good work on schedule.

- Process, planning, and preparation are all important, but they are subordinate to real results.

Useful Implementation Tools

This appendix contains a number of tools that can help you be more effective in forming a team, managing its progress, and handling typical problems. All the forms are adapted from Harvard ManageMentor®, an online product of Harvard Business School Publishing. For the convenience of readers, downloadable versions of these and other checklists, worksheet, and tools can be found on the Harvard Business Essentials series Web site: www.elearning.hbsp.org/businesstools. The four tools found in this appendix include:

1. **Defining Your Project (figure A–1).** This form will help you uncover the issues and parameters at the core of your project.

2. **Worksheet for Forming a Team (figure A–2).** Consider all aspects of your team—including members, skills, and resources—by completing this form.

3. **Checklist for Evaluating Whether a Group Is a Team (figure A–3).** This form will help you assess whether a group working together is indeed a team. Read the questions, and check off your answers.

4. **Project Progress Report (figure A–4).** You can use this form to report progress to the sponsor and other stakeholders, including team members.

FIGURE A-1

Defining Your Project

The "real" project

What is the perceived need or purpose for what we are trying to do?

What caused people to see this as a problem that needed to be solved?

What criteria are people going to use to judge this project as a success?

The stakeholders

Who has a stake in the solution or outcome?

How do the various stakeholders' goals for the project differ?

What functions or people might the project's activities or outcomes affect?

Who is going to contribute resources (people, space, time, tools, money)?

Skills required for the project

Skill needed	Possible team member
1.	1.
2.	2.
3.	3.
4.	4.
5.	5.
6.	6.

Source: Harvard ManageMentor® on Project Management (Boston: Harvard Business School Publishing, 1999).

FIGURE A-2

Worksheet for Forming a Team

Team purpose

Expected activities

Intended results

Available resources

Constraints

Necessary skills and qualities

Team members

Extent of decision-making authority (e.g., recommend or implement)

Duration

Source: Harvard ManageMentor® on Leading a Team (Boston: Harvard Business School Publishing, 1998).

FIGURE A-3

Checklist for Evaluating Whether a Group Is a Team

1. Is the group small enough in number to convene and communicate easily, to have open, interactive discussion, and to understand members' roles and responsibilities?

2. Do you have adequate levels of complementary skills in functional or technical areas, in problem solving and decision making, and in interpersonal capabilities?

3. Do you have a broad, meaningful purpose that all team members are committed to?

4. Do you have a set of agreed-upon performance goals?

5. Is the approach to doing the work clear and shared, making use of all team members' skills?

6. Do team members hold themselves individually and jointly accountable as measured against specific goals?

Source: Harvard ManageMentor® on Leading a Team (Boston: Harvard Business School Publishing, 1998).

FIGURE A-4

Project Progress Report

| Project: | Prepared by: |
| For the period from: | To: |

Current status

Key milestones for this period:

Achieved	Coming up next

Key issues or problems:

Resolved	Need to be resolved

Key decisions:

Made	Need to be made	By whom	When

Budget status:

Implications

Note any changes in objectives, timeline/delivery dates, project scope, and resource allocation (including people and financial).

Next steps

List the specific action steps that will be done to help move this project forward successfully. Put a name and date next to each step if possible.

Step	Person responsible	Date

Comments

Source: Harvard ManageMentor® on Project Management (Boston: Harvard Business School Publishing, 1999).

A Guide to Effective Coaching

Coaching is one of the contributions that leaders make to teams. Its aim is to help others improve their performance.

Begin with Observation

The first step in effective coaching is to understand the situation, the person, and his current skills. The best way to gain that understanding is through direct observation. Your goal should be to identify strengths and weaknesses and to understand the impact that the person's behavior has on coworkers and on his ability to achieve his goals. As you observe, keep these points in mind:

- **Learn what the person is doing or not doing well.** Be as precise as you can be, and try to get to the cause of problems. Consider this example:

  After observing several team meetings, the leader noted something about Harriet: She interrupted others frequently. This behavior appeared to prevent others from expressing their views. A less observant person might have said, "Harriet isn't a good team player." But that general statement would not have isolated Harriet's specific problem—a problem amenable to coaching.

- **Avoid premature judgments.** One or two observations may give an incomplete impression. So continue observing, particularly if you have any doubts about your perceptions.

- **Test your theories.** Where appropriate, discuss the situation with trusted peers or colleagues. Add their observations to your own.

- **Avoid unrealistic expectations.** Don't apply your own performance yardstick to others. You've probably progressed in your career by setting high expectations and achieving an outstanding track record. Assuming that others have identical motivations or identical strengths may be unrealistic and unfair.

- **Listen carefully.** A person may be asking for your help, but you may not be hearing him. Ask yourself, "Have I passed up chances to listen?" People don't always know what kind of help they need or exactly how to ask for it. When you see an opportunity, take the time to listen actively to direct reports.

Discuss Your Observations with the Other Person

Once you've determined where coaching can help, enter into dialogue with the person in question. But stick to observed behaviors. For example, begin by saying, "I've observed that you frequently interrupt other people during meetings." Also cite the impact of the person's behavior on group goals and on coworkers. For example, you might suggest, "If I were in one of your teammate's shoes, I'd interpret your habit of interrupting others as an attempt to dominate the meeting."

When describing behavior and its impact, be truthful and frank, yet supportive. Leave motives out of the discussion; doing otherwise will only make the person feel that he's under personal attack. Those motives would be pure speculation on your part in any case. Here's an example of an assumed motive: "Your inability to get reports done on time tells me that you don't like this type of work."

Be an Active Listener

As a coach, you must be highly tuned in to the other person. You do this through *active listening*. Active listening encourages communication and puts other people at ease. An active listener pays attention to the speaker by doing the following:

- Maintaining eye contact

- Smiling at appropriate moments

- Avoiding distractions

- Taking notes only if necessary

- Being sensitive to body language

- Listening first and evaluating later

- Never interrupting except to ask for clarification

- Indicating that he's listening by repeating what was said—for example, "So if I hear you right, you're having trouble with . . ."

Ask the Right Questions

Asking the right questions will help you understand the other person and determine his or her perspective. There are open-ended and closed questions. Each yields a different response.

Open-ended questions invite participation and idea sharing. Use them to:

- Explore alternatives: "What would happen if . . ."

- Uncover attitudes or needs: "How do you feel about our progress to date?"

- Establish priorities and allow elaboration: "What do you think the major issues are with this project?"

Closed questions lead to yes or no answers. Use them to:

- Focus the response: "Is the project on schedule?"

- Confirm what the other person has said: "So, your big problem is scheduling your time?"

When you want to find out more about the other person's motivations and feelings, use open-ended questions. Through this line of questioning, you may be able to uncover her views and deeper thoughts on the problem. This, in turn, will help you formulate better advice.

Begin Coaching

Once you understand the person and the situation, you can begin your coaching sessions.

Effective coaches offer ideas and advice in such a way that the person receiving them can hear them, respond to them, and consider their value. It is important to advocate your opinions in a clear and balanced way.

- Describe the individual's situation neutrally.

- State your opinion.

- Make the thoughts behind your opinion explicit.

- Share your own experiences if they might help.

- Encourage the other person to provide his or her perspective.

Your collaborations will be most successful if you use both inquiry and advocacy in your communication. Overreliance on inquiry can result in the participant's withholding important information and positions. Conversely, if you emphasize advocacy too heavily, you create a controlling atmosphere that can undermine the coaching partnership.

Give and Receive Feedback

Giving and receiving feedback is a critical part of coaching. This give-and-take goes on throughout the coaching process as you identify issues to work on, develop action plans together, and assess the results. Here are a few tips for giving feedback:

- Focus on behavior—not character, attitudes, or personality.

- Describe the other person's behavior and its impact on projects and/or teammates, but avoid judgmental language that will put that person on the defensive. For example, instead of saying, "You're rude and domineering," say, "You interrupted Fred several times during each of our last three meetings."

- Avoid generalizations. Instead of saying, "You did a really good job," offer something more specific, such as, "The transparencies you used for your presentation were effective in getting the message across."

- Be sincere. Give feedback with the clear intent of helping the person improve.

- Be realistic. Focus on factors that the other person can control.

- Give feedback early and often in the coaching process. Frequent feedback that is delivered soon after the fact is more effective than infrequent feedback.

You also need to be open to feedback on how effective you are as a coach. Coaches who are able to request and process feedback about themselves learn more about the effectiveness of their management styles and create greater trust. To improve your ability to receive feedback, ask for specific information. For example, ask, "What did I say that made you think I wasn't interested in your proposal?" or "How were my suggestions helpful to you?"

When you ask for clarification, do so in a way that doesn't put the other person on the defensive. Instead of saying, "What do you mean I seemed hostile to your idea?" say, "Could you give me an example?" Also:

- Be willing to receive both negative and positive feedback.

- Encourage the other person to avoid emotion-laden terms. For example, try this approach: "You said that I am often inflexible. Give me an example of things I do that give you the sense that I am not flexible."

And be sure to thank the person for his or her feedback, both positive and negative. Doing so will improve trust and model productive behavior to the person you are coaching.

Many organizations use 360-degree feedback programs to prompt team members to provide honest feedback to one another, and especially to the team leader. This type of feedback can increase "interpersonal congruence," or the extent to which self-assessments are congruent with other people's appraisals—something that supports team effectiveness.

Develop an Action Plan

Some coaching situations benefit from an action plan. A situation in which a person must bring his performance up to standard within a certain time or risk dismissal is one clear example. Another is when you have an excellent teammate you want to prepare for a higher-level job within a few months. In each case, a plan assures systematic attention to performance improvement.

An action plan should be written by the person being coached and should describe the specific changes in behavior or new skills the person must work on. Like any effective plan, it should include a timetable and measures of success. Your role in creating the plan should include:

- Ensuring that the goals are realistic

- Helping the person prioritize the tasks needed to achieve those goals

- Highlighting potential obstacles and brainstorming potential solutions

- Determining what additional coaching support or training will be required.

Work together on these agreements. Your involvement will demonstrate your interest in the person's success and your commitment to the action plan.

Always Follow Up

Effective coaching includes follow-up that checks progress and helps individuals continue to improve. Your follow-up might include:

- Asking what is going well and what is not

- Sharing your observations and reinforcing positive progress

- Looking for opportunities for continued coaching and feedback

- Identifying possible modifications to the action plan

- Asking what about the coaching session was helpful and what could be improved

If you're a new manager, or new to coaching, your first efforts may be feel uncomfortable and may not be entirely effective. Just remember that you will get better with practice.

SOURCE: Adapted from Harvard ManageMentor® on Coaching.

Team Troubleshooting Guide

Problem	Characteristic behavior	Try this
Unhealthy Conflict	• Personal attacks • Sarcasm • Some members shut down in face of heated discussion • Dialogue argumentative • Absence of expressions of support for others' views • Aggressive gesturing	• Interrupt personal attacks or sarcasm • Ask members to describe behavior, rather than attack character • Encourage all members to express views • Review or create norms about discussing contentious topics
Trouble Reaching Consensus	• Holding onto positions regardless of others' input • Same argument continues to be repeated with no new information • No one formally closes the discussion	• Solicit input on members' key interests and needs • Discuss consequences of not reaching consensus • Ask what needs to happen in order to complete discussion
Team Isn't Communicating Well	• Members interrupt or talk over others • Some members are excessively quiet • Problems are hinted at but never formally addressed • Members assume meanings without asking for clarification • Nonverbal signals are at odds with what's being said	• Review or create group norms for discussion • Actively solicit all members' views • Routinely ask members to be specific and give examples • Address nonverbal signals that are at odds with verbal content • Consider using an outside facilitator
Lack of Progress	• Meetings seem like a waste of time • Action items are not completed on time • Closed issues continue to be revisited	• Restate direction and assess what is left to accomplish • Ask members to identify causes of late work and brainstorm solutions • Leader should discourage revisiting closed issues by reminding team of previous decisions and focusing on next steps

Problem	Characteristic behavior	Try this
Low Participation	• Assignments are not completed • Poor attendance • Low energy at meetings	• Confirm that leader's expectations for participation are shared by other members • Solicit members' views on reasons for low involvement • Develop a plan to address reasons for low participation • Assess fit of members to team tasks
Unclear Goals	• Individual member(s) promote outcome that is in conflict with the team goals • Team members capitulate too quickly in discussions • Team is spending an inordinate amount of time discussing actions that are not aligned with the team goals	• Remind members of team goals during each meeting • Ask how each action being discussed will contribute to the team's goals • Be suspicious of premature agreement. Ask members to play "devil's advocate" about issues around which everyone quickly agrees
Inept Leadership	• Leader does not solicit enough involvement from team members • Leader does all the work • Team falls behind • Conflicts become unhealthy • Lack of vision • Leadership perspective is myopic; it represents one area rather than full constituency	• Be brave: Meet with leader to express concerns about perceived leadership deficiency • Consider how you might help leader to be more effective—e.g., volunteer for additional tasks • If leadership problems persist, express concerns to sponsor

Lack of Management Support	• Work of team is rejected by management
	• Senior managers express discomfort about the team's work
	• Necessary resources are not provided
		• One of several preventable problems has occurred:
		  • Team does not have an adequate sponsor
		  • Sponsor has not "signed off" on goals and resources
		  • Team sponsor and/or other stakeholders have not been adequately informed of team progress
		• Work with sponsors to clarify team charter and resources

Lack of Resources	• Team "work" assignments are not coupled with a trade-off from regular job responsibilities • No budget for necessary materials or outside participation	• Negotiate trade-offs with sponsor and members' supervisors • Negotiate for budget • If sponsors and stakeholders will not contract for needed time or resources, team success is unlikely; consider disbanding the team
Don't Know What's Wrong		• Contact human resources for consulting help

Notes

Chapter 1

1. J. Richard Hackman, *Leading Teams: Setting the Stage for Great Performances* (Boston: Harvard Business School Press, 2002), 41.

2. Ibid., 42–43.

3. Jeffrey T. Polzer, "Leading Teams," Class note N9-403-094 (Boston: Harvard Business School, 2002), 3–5. This class note draws on research by Polzer and many other scholars.

Chapter 2

1. Jon R. Katzenbach and Douglas K. Smith, *The Wisdom of Teams: Creating the High-Performance Organization* (Boston: Harvard Business School Press, 1993).

2. J. Richard Hackman, *Leading Teams: Setting the Stage for Great Performances* (Boston: Harvard Business School Press, 2002).

Chapter 3

1. Michael Wachter, *8 Lies of Teamwork* (Avon Lake, OH: CorporateImpact, 2002), 60.

2. Richard Leifer, Christopher McDermott, Gina Colarelli O'Connor, Lois Peters, Mark Rice, and Robert Veryzer, *Radical Innovation: How Mature Companies Can Outsmart Upstarts* (Boston: Harvard Business School Press, 2000), 163.

3. Niccolò Machiavelli, *The Prince*, available at <http://www.bibliomania.com> (accessed 19 September, 2003), chapter 6.

4. Bernard DeVoto, ed., *The Journals of Lewis and Clark* (Boston: Houghton Mifflin Company, 1953), lii–liii.

5. Stephen E. Ambrose, *Undaunted Courage: Meriwether Lewis, Thomas Jefferson, and the Opening of the American West* (New York: Simon & Schuster, 1996), 117–118.

6. Gregory H. Watson, *Strategic Benchmarking: How to Rate Your Company's Performance against the World's Best* (New York: John Wiley & Sons, Inc., 1993), 114–115.

7. Jeffrey T. Polzer, "Leading Teams," Class note N9-403-094 (Boston: Harvard Business School, 2002), 7.

8. Jon R. Katzenbach and Douglas K. Smith, "The Wisdom of Teams," *Harvard Business Review*, March–April 1993, 118.

9. ———, *The Wisdom of Teams: Creating the High-Performance Organization* (Boston: Harvard Business School Press, 1993), 62.

10. J. Richard Hackman, *Leading Teams: Setting the Stage for Great Performances* (Boston: Harvard Business School Press, 2002), 83.

11. Ibid., 74.

Chapter 4

1. Jon R. Katzenbach and Douglas K. Smith, "The Discipline of Teams," *Harvard Business Review*, March–April 1993, 118.

2. Michael Wachter, *8 Lies of Teamwork* (Avon Lake, OH: Corporate-Impact, 2002), 77.

3. J. Richard Hackman, *Leading Teams: Setting the Stage for Great Performances* (Boston: Harvard Business School Press, 2002), 87.

4. See Turid Horgen, Donald A. Schon, William L. Porter, and Michael L. Joroff, *Excellence by Design: Transforming Workplace and Work Practice* (New York: John Wiley & Sons, Inc., 1998).

5. Thomas J. Allen, "Communication Networks in R&D Labs," *R&D Management* 1 (1971): 14–21.

6. Marc H. Meyer and Alvin P. Lehnerd, *The Power of Product Platforms: Building Value and Cost Leadership* (New York: Free Press, 1997), 137.

7. Katzenbach and Smith, "The Discipline of Teams," 118.

Chapter 5

1. Gregory H. Watson, *Strategic Benchmarking: How to Rate Your Company's Performance against the World's Best* (New York: John Wiley & Sons, Inc., 1993), 113–117.

2. J. Richard Hackman, *Leading Teams: Setting the Stage for Great Performances* (Boston: Harvard Business School Press, 2002), 205.

3. Jon R. Katzenbach and Douglas K. Smith, "The Discipline of Teams," *Harvard Business Review*, March–April 1993, 116.

4. Jeffrey T. Polzer, "Leading Teams," Class note N9-403-094 (Boston: Harvard Business School, 2002), 17–18.

5. Adapted from Harvard ManageMentor® on Creativity.

6. Dorothy Leonard and Walter Swap, *When Sparks Fly: Igniting Creativity in Groups* (Boston: Harvard Business School Press, 1999), 6.

Chapter 6

1. Jeffrey T. Polzer, "Leading Teams," Class note N9-403-094 (Boston: Harvard Business School, 2002), 15.

2. This section is adapted from Harvard ManageMentor® on Leading Teams.

3. Shawn L. Berman, Jonathan Down, and Charles W. L. Hill, "Tacit Knowledge As a Source of Competitive Advantage in the National Basketball Association," *Academy of Management Journal*, 45, no. 1 (2000): 18.

4. J. Richard Hackman, *Leading Teams: Setting the Stage for Great Performances* (Boston: Harvard Business School Press, 2002), 27.

5. Amy Edmondon, Richard Bohmer, and Gary Pisano, "Speeding Up Team Learning," *Harvard Business Review*, October 2001, 6.

Chapter 7

1. This chapter is adapted from Harvard ManageMentor® on Virtual Teams

2. Gary M. Olson and Judith S. Olson, "Distance Matters," *Human Computer Interactions*, 15 (2000): 141.

Chapter 8

1. Morten Hansen, "FT Summer School Day 4—Knowledge Management," *Financial Times*, 8 August 2002, 14.

2. John C. Maxwell, *The 17 Essential Qualities of a Team Player: Becoming the Kind of Person Every Team Wants* (Nashville: Thomas Nelson Publishers, 2002), 25.

3. Robert H. Schaffer and Harvey A. Thomson, "Successful Change Programs Begin with Results," *Harvard Business Review*, January–February 1992, 80–89.

Glossary

CHARTER   A concise written description of the team's intended work. The charter may contain the name of the sponsor, a timetable, a description of deliverables and benefits to the company, and a budget.

COACHING   A two-way activity in which the parties share knowledge and experience in order to maximize a team member's potential and help him or her achieve agreed-upon goals.

CONVERGENT THINKING   A mode of thinking that evaluates ideas to determine which are genuinely novel and worth pursuing. It channels the results of divergent thinking into a concrete proposal for action.

DIVERGENT THINKING   A mode of thinking in which an individual or group breaks away from familiar or established ways of seeing and doing and views old things in new ways.

FACILITATOR   As applied to team-based work, a person with special training in helping people communicate and collaborate. Facilitators are generally outside consultants. They do not involve themselves with team tasks but provide expert technical advice or help.

FREE RIDERS   Team members who obtain the benefits of membership without doing their share.

GROUPWARE   Software applications that help people work together.

INTERPERSONAL SKILL   The ability to work effectively and harmoniously with others and to engage in constructive debate.

ORGANIZATIONAL SKILL   The ability to communicate and share resources with other units of the company.

PROJECT MANAGEMENT   A process for overseeing a focused, goal-oriented effort from start to finish, involving the allocation of people and resources, coordinating activities and resource expenditures, and monitoring performance. The typical project has four phases: planning, buildup, implementation, and phaseout.

PROJECT PLAN   A team charter, but with more detail about tasks, milestones, deliverables, risks, and timetables.

PROJECT TEAM   A team organized around a nonroutine task of limited duration.

SELF-MANAGED WORK TEAM   A small group of people that is empowered to handle a particular ongoing task. In many cases, the team selects its leader and new members and may even have the authority to discharge members who fail to meet team standards.

TEAM   A small number of individuals with complementary skills who are committed to a common goal for which they hold themselves collectively accountable.

TEAM CHARTER   See *Charter*.

TEAM PROCESSES   Collaboration and information sharing among team members.

TECHNICAL SKILL   Expertise in a particular discipline or activity, such as engineering, software programming, or finance.

VIRTUAL TEAM   A team that, for the most part, is linked through communications that are not face-to-face: e-mail, voice mail, telephone, groupware, and videoconferencing.

WORK GROUP   A leader-manager with two or more employees. Interactions occur between each work group member and the leader-manager; employees do not interact with each other in completing their tasks.

For Further Reading

General

Harvard Business School Publishing. *The Art of Managing Effective Teams. Harvard Management Update* Collection. Boston: Harvard Business School Publishing, 1999. This comprehensive collection from the editors of the *Harvard Management Update* newsletter provides you with all the expert ideas, insights, and solutions you need to help your teams succeed.

Jassawalla, Aran R., and Hemant C. Sashittal. "Strategies of Effective New Product Team Leaders." *California Management Review*, January 2000. This article looks specifically at new-product teams. Most leaders of such teams are aware of the complexity of the task they face and the changes that must occur before cross-functional teams can accelerate the product-development process. Yet few team leaders consistently act on these insights and effect meaningful change. This article reveals the secrets to effective product-team leadership.

Jones, Steven D., Michael M. Beyerlein, and Jack J. Phillips, eds. *In Action: Developing High-Performance Work Teams.* Vol. 1. Alexandria, VA: American Society for Training & Development, 1999. In this book, fourteen case studies present a variety of approaches to implementing teams in the workplace—including the unique configurations that come with virtual teams. It includes guidelines for moving from supervisor to team manager.

Katzenbach, Jon R., and Douglas K. Smith. "The Discipline of Teams." *Harvard Business Review* OnPoint Enhanced Edition. Boston: Harvard Business School Publishing, 2000. The essence of a team is shared commitment. Without it, groups perform as individuals; with it, they become a unit of collective performance. The fundamental distinction between teams and other forms of working groups turns on performance. A working group relies on the individual contributions of its

161

members for group performance. But a team strives for something greater than its members could achieve individually. The best teams invest a tremendous amount of time shaping a purpose, and they translate their purpose into specific performance goals. Team members also pitch in and become accountable with and to their teammates. The authors identify three basic types of teams: teams that recommend things, teams that make or do things, and teams that run things. The key is knowing where in the organization real teams should be encouraged. Team potential exists anywhere hierarchy or organizational boundaries inhibit good performance.

The same authors develop their ideas more fully in *The Wisdom of Teams: Creating the High-Performance Organization*. Boston: Harvard Business School Press, 1993.

Parcells, Bill. "The Tough Work of Turning Around a Team." *Harvard Business Review*, November–December 2000. How do you reverse the fortunes of a troubled team? Bill Parcells—one of the National Football League's most successful coaches—offers managers three rules: (1) Make it clear from day one that you're in charge, (2) view confrontation as healthy, and (3) identify small goals and hit them. As Parcells maintains, if you get people on your team who share the same goals and passion— and then push them to achieve their highest potential—the team is bound to come out on top.

Wellins, Richard S., Dick Schaaf, and Kathy Harper Shomo. *Succeeding with Teams: 101 Tips That Really Work*. Minneapolis: Lakewood Books, 1994. This book is aimed at all those involved in the evolution of teams, wherever they may be in the process. It offers a variety of tips for achieving success with teams. Chapter topics range from assessing your team's readiness to clarifying roles and responsibilities to setting goals and chartering the team. Information is presented in a clear, concise format, making this text a good choice for those seeking a quick reference and easily digested information.

Virtual Teams

Harvard Business School Publishing. "Communicating with Virtual Project Teams." *Harvard Management Communication Letter*, December 2000. How do you bring a project team together when its members are spread over several continents and time zones? Enter a new breed of Internet-based products called "virtual work spaces." These products offer a password-protected site, with services ranging from e-mail and information storage to chat rooms and scheduling. This article describes some of the pros and cons of such services and lists Web site addresses to help you learn more about them.

Harvard Business School Publishing. "Creating Successful Virtual Organizations." *Harvard Management Communication Letter*, December 2000. In many ways, the world of work is entirely different than it was just a decade ago. You work with people you never see—and may have never even met. Your colleagues come and go at all hours and in all manner of dress, and they may not even be actual employees of the same company. This complexity adds up to one thing: Good communication is more difficult—and more necessary—than ever. This article turns to the experts for some ground rules on communication in the virtual age.

Kiser, Kim. "Working on World Time." *Training*, March 1999. Kiser examines issues such as building trust and learning how to use technology in the context of a virtual team.

Lipnack, Jessica, and Jeffrey Stamps. *Virtual Teams: Reaching Across Space, Time, and Organizations with Technology*. New York: John Wiley & Sons, Inc., 1997. In this clear and comprehensive guide, Lipnack and Stamps take the reader through all the elements of setting up and maintaining a virtual team. Included are the basic principles of people, purpose, and links; technology considerations; and communication strategies. The authors describe the special challenges of virtual teams and offer suggestions about how to meet them.

Malone, Thomas W., and Robert J. Laubacher. "The Dawn of the E-Lance Economy." *Harvard Business Review*, September–October 1998. In the age of virtual teams, you and your team may well find yourselves working with "e-lancers" at times—independent contractors who are connected through personal computers and electronic networks and who join together in fluid and temporary networks to produce and sell their goods and services to clients. This article explores how e-lancing promises to overturn the old rules of business and even render big, traditional companies obsolete. In many ways, the e-lance economy is already upon us—as evidenced by the rise in outsourcing and telecommuting, in the increasing importance of ad hoc project teams, and in the evolution of the Internet. Many of the building blocks necessary to this new economy are already in place as well—including efficient networks, data-interchange standards, groupware, and electronic currency. The authors examine the opportunities and the challenges that may arise in such an economy and describe fundamental changes that may reshape team leaders' roles.

Maruca, Regina Fazio. "How Do You Manage an Off-Site Team?" *Harvard Business Review* OnPoint Enhanced Edition. Boston: Harvard Business School Publishing, 2000. In this fictitious case study, *HBR* editor Regina F. Maruca explores the challenges of managing employees in the alternative workplace. Allison Scher is threatening to quit. Penny Ryan wants to run the team. The manager of these off-site workers, Craig Bedell, feels blindsided by their conflict. And the whole mess has Maggie Pinto, the head of HR, wondering whether she should cancel the company-wide rollout of the telecommuting program. How did this situation get to the boiling point so quickly? Four commentators offer their advice on how the company can patch up the short-term problem and lay the foundation for a successful future.

Index

accountability in teams, 77–78
Allen, Tom, 60

being a team player
  commitment and, 135
  openness to different ways of
    working, 130–131
  openness to new ideas, 129–130
  reliability and, 135–136
  results-orientation importance,
    136–137
  seeking alternatives, 132
  sharing knowledge, 131–132
  summary, 137–138
  win-win solutions goal,
    134–135
  working relationships and, 133
Bohner, Richard, 101
Bourgeois, L. J. III, 94
budget development, 57–58

charter, team, 39–42
Clark, William, xii, 30
coaching
  action plan development, 150
  active listening, 146–147
  beginning the process, 148
  feedback and, 148–150

follow-up, 151
  observation and, 145–146
  questions to ask, 147–148
  team leaders and, 72–74
  virtual teams and, 122–123
collaboration
  collaborative behavior, 93, 95
  collaborative leadership, 75
  facilitation of, 58–62
  virtual teams and, 120
commitment
  being a team player and, 135
  rewards and, 20
  team characteristics and, 17–20
  virtual teams and, 119–120
compatibility problems and virtual
  teams, 114
conflict management, 86–88, 94–97
convergent thinking, 85–86
Corps of Discovery, xi–xiii, 17–18,
  30
creativity on teams. See team
  creativity
culture issues on virtual teams,
  121–122

database access and virtual teams,
  112
data silos, 97–98

decision making on a team
    approaches, 50–51
    consensus and, 51
    procedures' importance, 50
    sponsor's authority and, 49
DeVoto, Bernard, 30
divergent thinking, 84–85

Economy, Peter, 75
Edison, Thomas, 36
Edmondon, Amy, 101
Eisenhardt, Kathleen, 94
e-mail and virtual teams, 110–111

facilitator on a team, 39
fax machines and virtual teams,
    112–113
FIZ (*Forschungs und Innovationszen-
    trum*), 59–60
forming teams
    choosing a leader, 29–31
    leader's roles, 29
    member selection (*see* members
        of a team)
    purposes for forming, 5
    team sponsor, 27–29
    worksheet for, 141f

Gantt chart, 99t
glossary, 161–162
groupthink, 80–82
groupware and virtual teams,
    112

Hackman, J. Richard, 4, 41, 57, 72,
    101
Hansen, Morten, 133

identity of the team. *See* team
    identity
information sharing, 97–98
Insomnia Brigade, 36
intranet sites and virtual teams, 111

Janus, Irving, 80

Kahwajy, Jean, 94
Katzenbach, Jon R., 14, 38, 47, 63,
    77

launch meeting
    goals for, 47–48
    physical presence importance,
        46–47
    sponsor's presence importance,
        47
leader, team. *See* team leader
Leading Teams (Hackman), 4
learning, team, 100–103
Lehnerd, Al, 60
Leonard, Dorothy, 84
Lewis, Meriwether, xii–xiii, 17, 30
Lewis and Clark. *See* William
    Clark; Meriwether Lewis

management of a team. *See* project
    management; team leader
Maxwell, John, 135
members of a team
    adding and subtracting, 37
    choosing, 32–33
    optimal team size, 38
    skill assessment, 34–37
    team players (*see* being a team
        player)

to-do list, 38
Meyer, Marc, 60

norms of behavior for teams,
    62–64

Olson, Gary, 115
Olson, Judith, 115
operating as a team. *See* team
    processes

PERT (Performance Evaluation
    and Review Technique), 53,
    56f
Pisano, Gary, 101
Polzer, Jeffrey, 8, 9, 10, 35, 36, 78,
    95
project management
    objectives clarification, 52
    progress report worksheet, 143f
    project definition worksheet, 140
    scheduling tips, 55
    tasks assignment, 55–56
    tasks specification, 53, 54t, 56f
project teams, 6

rewards
    behavior alignment using, 42–43
    commitment and, 20
    supportive environment and, 22
    from team work, 21
Ribbink, Kim, 121

Schaffer, Robert, 136
Seifter, Harvey, 75
self-managed teams, 5–6

Smith, Douglas K., 14, 38, 47, 63,
    77
sponsor, team, 27–29, 47
SPORG (Space and Organization
    Research Group), 59
Strategic Benchmarking (Watson), 34
Swap, Walter, 84

team characteristics
    alignment with the organization,
        22–23
    behavior alignment through re-
        wards, 42–43
    charter, 39–42
    checklist for, 142
    clear, common, measurable goal,
        15–17
    commitment to the goal, 17–20
    competence, 14–15
    of a creative team, 83, 84t
    facilitator, 39
    member contribution and bene-
        fits, 20–21
    summary, 24, 43–44
    supportive environment need,
        21–22
    uncommitted members and, 19
team creativity
    benefits of diversity, 82–83
    characteristics of a creative team,
        83, 84t
    divergent and convergent think-
        ing, 84–86
team identity
    benefits of, 77–78
    establishing for virtual teams,
        118–119
    fostering, 78–80
team leader
    being a learning leader, 102

team leader (*continued*)
  choosing, 29–31
  as coach, 72
  collaborative leadership and, 75
  conflict management, 86–88
  divergent and convergent think-
    ing management, 84–86
  duties, 20–21
  fostering a team identity, 78–80
  groupthink avoidance, 82
  informal leaders, 74, 76
  as initiator, 69–70
  managing versus coaching, 73
  as model, 70–71
  as negotiator, 71–72
  roles, 29, 68–69
  summary, 89
  team creativity and, 82–83, 84t
team learning, 100–103
team players. *See* being a team
    player
team processes
  collaborative behavior, 93, 95
  conflict, defusing, 95–97
  conflict, healthy, 94
  defined, 93
  evaluating performance of indi-
    vidual members, 105–106
  evaluation methods, 104–105
  information sharing, 97–98
  keeping on schedule, 100
  process factors to measure,
    103–104, 142
  small wins for motivation, 98–99
  summary, 106
  team learning and success,
    100–103
team room
  setting up, 60–62
  for virtual teams, 111
teams

benefits and costs, 7–8
characteristics of (*see* team char-
    acteristics)
checklist for evaluating co-
    herency, 142
decision making on, 49–51
features of, 4
forming (*see* forming teams)
members (*see* members of a
    team)
need for, 7
process or operation (*see* team
    processes)
project, 6
purposes for forming, 5
self-managed, 5–6
summary, 10–11
use or don't use decision, 8–10
virtual (*see* virtual teams)
work groups versus, 3–4, 142f
team start-up
  budget development, 57–58
  collaboration facilitation, 58–62
  decision-making consensus,
    49–51
  launch meeting, 46–48
  norms of behavior establishment,
    62–64
  success definition, 56–57
  summary, 64–65
  work plan (*see* project manage-
    ment)
telephone conferencing and virtual
    teams, 114–115
text-editing software and virtual
    teams, 113–114
Thomson, Harvey, 136

videoconferencing and virtual
    teams, 115

virtual teams
  benefits and challenges, 108–109
  coaching, 122–123
  collaboration facilitation, 120
  commitment and, 119–120
  culture issues, 121–122
  summary, 124–125
  team identity establishment,
    118–119
  technical issues (*see* virtual team
    technology)
  tips for a good start, 123–124
virtual team technology
  compatibility problems, 114
  database access, 112
  decisions concerning, 116–117
  e-mail, 110–111
  fax machines, 112–113

  groupware, 112
  intranet sites, 111
  telephone conferencing,
    114–115
  text-editing software, 113–114
  videoconferencing, 115
  Web sites, 111
  whiteboards, 116

Wachter, Michael, 27
Watson, Gregory, 34
Web sites and virtual teams, 111
whiteboards and virtual teams, 116
The Wisdom of Teams (Katzenbach
  and Smith), 14
work-group model, 2–4

About the Subject Adviser

JEFFREY T. POLZER is an associate professor of organizational behavior at Harvard Business School (HBS). His research investigates a variety of factors that improve team performance. He also studies how group affiliations affect people's decisions, perceptions, and social interactions, especially in diverse work teams. Professor Polzer has published his work in a variety of top management journals and was recognized by the Academy of Management for writing the top article on organizational behavior in 2002.

Professor Polzer teaches the second-year M.B.A. course Leading Teams and the doctoral course Human Behavior at HBS, where he previously taught the required M.B.A. course Leadership and Organizational Behavior. Before coming to Harvard, he taught at the University of Texas at Austin and Northwestern University, where he earned his doctoral degree at the Kellogg Graduate School of Management. He has conducted a variety of executive training sessions at those schools.

About the Writer

RICHARD LUECKE is the writer of this and several other books in the Harvard Business Essentials series. Based in Salem, Massachusetts, Mr. Luecke has authored or developed more than thirty book and dozens of articles on a wide range of business subjects. He has an M.B.A. from the University of St. Thomas.